THE LESS EXPENSIVE

SPREAD

THE LESS EXPENSIVE

SPREAD

Delights & Dilemmas of a Weekend Cowboy

IRVING TOWNSEND

J. N. TOWNSEND PUBLISHING

EXETER, NEW HAMPSHIRE

Copyright 1990 J. N. Townsend Publishing

Published by
J. N. Townsend Publishing
12 Greenleaf Drive
Exeter, NH 03833

Original hardcover edition published by Dial Press, 1971.

This book was typeset on a Macintosh Plus using Aldus
PageMaker, International English V2.0a by Heidi Fernald.

Printed in the United States of America.

First Printing.

Library of Congress Cataloging-in-Publication Data

Townsend, Irving, 1920-1981.
    The less expensive spread: delights and dilemmas of a
weekend cowboy/Irving Townsend
        p.   cm.

1. Townsend, Irving, 1920-1981. 2. New Englanders--California--
Biography. 3. Ranchers--California--Santa Ynez Valley--
Biography. 4. American wit and humor. 5. Businessmen--
California--biography.
I. Title

CT275.T7494A3 1989   979.4'91--dc19   [B]   88-24911
CIP

ISBN 0-9617426-3-1

Cover illustration by Judith Roberts-Rondeau.

For my family

and the animals

Also by Irving Townsend

Separate Lifetimes

On Record: The John Hammond Story

1

"I would rather sit on a pumpkin
and have it all to myself
than be crowded on a velvet pillow."
- THOREAU

I am the most recent member of a long line of Townsends who for generations have refused to leave New England. No wagon trains for us, drinking out of dippers and being told by Ward Bond to "find cover." We have proudly walked up and down the furrows of the same fields for a hundred years or so, then, for another hundred years, marched off to the factory every morning swinging our lunch pails. The West and the world have always ended for us at the Berkshires.

So I wasn't advised to go West. My boss told me to go. I didn't decide. It was decided for me. So much for my pioneering instinct. But once the West had become inevitable it seemed to us the only sensible thing to do. My oldest daughter Susie, nine years old when we moved west and born with a crippling bone disease,

1

would have the advantages of new research at the University of California at Los Angeles. While no cure was then known, we felt encouraged by what we had heard about bone specialists in the West. And then there was the climate. Fewer colds per child. No more ski suits or lost mittens. Perhaps, no more mayflies and mosquitos.

Before we moved to California I was living with my family on a farm outside of Westport, Connecticut, and commuting a hundred miles a day back and forth to New York City. I was then, as I still am, working for a major recording company which had decided it needed a West Coast office with me in it. Our family consisted then of my wife, Freddie, three daughters (and another away at college), two collies and a cat, two goats, and a horse called Chestnut. I count only permanent members. Turtles, mice, wounded birds and fish, as we all know, come and go. When the word came to move, we decided, after considerable discussion, to leave the goats and Chestnut behind and set about finding good homes for them. As is often the case with animals in my household, ours were unaware that they were animals at all. I am not exactly Clyde Beatty when it comes to training, and my horse was a good example.

In my six years with Chestnut I had become his valet. I began by riding him across the fields on weekends and ended up following behind him with a shovel. He did not like to leave his barn, so our ride began reluctantly and continued until I had needled him as far as the stone wall at the end of the field. The return trip at full gallop was an experience beyond my abilities as a horseman, and I clung to his neck in panic as we ground to a halt at the stable door, crouched as he entered, and slid to the floor exhausted. After a few of these scenic rides I decided to contain my urge to tour my acres and devoted Saturdays to cleaning and feeding and brushing him by the hour. I carried pails of water to him morning and evening, summer and winter. I whitewashed his stable and kept his straw fresh. And, as I say, followed him out into his pasture with my shovel and wheelbarrow, picking up his droppings almost before they dropped. He didn't seem to like me any better for all of this.

2

Once, during a severe blizzard, I shut him in the barn to keep out drifting snow and wind. When I went out to bring him his pail of water, I opened the door again and out he flew, kicking me in the chest as he plunged into the drifts. He grew so fat I could not have put his saddle on anyway. He used to sleep full length all afternoon in the pasture while I watched Westerns in the house, and once I was disturbed by a concerned motorist who stopped, rang my doorbell, and announced that there was a dead horse in my field. "You must have been drinking," I snapped. But I checked on him; there he was, the fattest horse in Connecticut, snoring in the grass.

Finding a home for Chestnut was no easy matter, so I turned the job over to Freddie. And, by God, she found one. His new owners came over one Saturday and stood outside the stable admiring him. He didn't even look at them. They had difficulty pulling him out, but as usual we were there with carrots and apples and lumps of sugar, and Chestnut was rewarded for each step he took. I think they planned to ride him home, which of course was ridiculous, but by holding apples just beyond his nose all the way down the road, they did manage to walk him away. They paid us two hundred dollars, with saddle, bridle, and toiletry articles thrown in. Before they could lead him back again we were on our way to California.

Finding a home for a large white goat named Camille and her small son Cashmere was much more difficult, not only because people have the wrong idea about goats, but also because, as Freddie read somewhere, you have to be careful of Italians. Goats, contrary to popular opinion, don't eat tin cans, or for that matter, anything dirty at all (I even had to wash their apples for them), but Italians, she said, eat goats. She spent the day advertising and investigating the ancestry of anyone interested in two free goats, and somehow found a couple who "just loved goats," and who were not, apparently, Italian. We never did find out what had happened to the goats they loved so much, but their delight with ours convinced my wife and off we went one Saturday morning to deliver Camille and Cashmere.

Doing anything with a large goat in a small space is difficult.

Four sharp hooves and a very knobby head, all resisting, are not easy to cope with. (I'll never understand how Robert Benchley wrapped a goat as a gift.) But I thought I had solved the problem when I filled the back of our station wagon with hay, pushed and shoved the two goats on top of it, and drove up Route 7 to their new home. Traffic along that two-lane New England artery was heavy as always, but the goats were beginning to enjoy the ride when, of course, I had a flat tire.

There was little room to pull off that road, and what room there was was a sloping shoulder of asphalt. Changing a tire under the best of circumstances is not one of my talents, and the prospect of changing a tire on an incline off a busy highway shook what little confidence I had. Moreover, as I suddenly remembered, the spare and all the tools in that station wagon were under the goats. There was nothing to do but give orders.

"Get the goats out," I shouted, "and keep them out of traffic. I'll get the hay out and find the jack."

Freddie ran around and pulled both goats out of the wagon by their chains. They pulled the other way, as they always did, but she finally landed at the side of the road, wrapped in long chains, the goats within inches of the stream of cars. I piled their hay behind the car and dug for the tools and spare beneath the floor, breathing hard and certain that this sort of thing could never happen to anyone but me.

"Can you jack it up on this slope?" Freddie asked.

"I don't know."

"I can't help. The chains are wound around my ankles."

"Just keep the damn goats from butting me."

"They're just being playful," she said. "This is exciting for them."

"I wish you'd found a hungry Italian," I muttered.

I managed to jack up the left rear wheel, cars whistling by, the wrench lost in the hay pile, the goats nibbling foliage beside the road. Finally the job was done and we stuffed the hay and goats back into the wagon and resumed our trip to the goat lady. She and her husband met us at their gate, the woman clapping her hands in

4

delight, the man, I thought, somewhat less enthusiastic.

"Oh, we'll be so glad to have them," she exclaimed. "We've missed ours so much!"

She led them into her yard where they headed for her roses, dragging her helplessly behind the chains.

"I hope you really like goats," Freddie said to her husband, a little wistfully.

"My wife does," he answered.

"You're sure you won't eat them or anything," Freddie continued. "They're pets," she added.

"Eat a goat?" He looked at her amazed. "She does the cooking, and she won't eat no goat."

Reassured and anxious to leave while the goats were busy with the roses, we drove away, back to our packing. We didn't speak. Leaving an animal behind is never an easy thing to do, and I think we were both remembering the day Cashmere was born in the garage while Freddie and our neighbors toasted him with martinis and I cleaned the stall. The garage was empty now, and I was glad we were heading west. But I was secretly proud of myself too. Maybe John Wayne could change a broken wagon wheel for the schoolmarm while Hollywood Indians were shooting flaming arrows into her wagon, but could he change a tire on Route 7 under all those conditions? Perhaps I was ready for the West after all.

Our trip to California by jet with Susie, who had a broken leg, Jeremy, who tossed balloons into sleeping passengers' laps while Nicole ran to retrieve them, and our collies and cat in boxes in the cargo section, was uneventful. We had, of course, been there before and had bought a house in West Los Angeles "because it has more trees," but it was not until we actually moved in that I discovered that most of Los Angeles is neither city nor country but a giant suburbia. Houses costing more than my farm are crowded together, their tiny lawns immaculate, their occupants proud of their mortgages and their pools, watering and spreading Snarol. Nothing grows in Los Angeles without permission from the owner, and the lifted hind leg of a dog is punishable by fine, imprisonment, or both.

Our house was like the rest: picture windows revealing pictures I didn't want to look at, pool and patio backyard in chlorine blue and sunbaked white, screened from neighbors' eyes by vines and fences, but within easy earshot of arguments over barbecues and one-sided telephone conversations, grass and semitropical plants allowed to grow, but not too much, ground cover encouraged to prevent fires, blue and pink spotlights to ensure Technicolor moonlight, a formal, fettered garden fifty miles across. Where was the West I had watched on television back East? I knew it was out here somewhere, but not in Los Angeles. My gentle collie, Amber was chased home by a shouting neighbor, who threatened to call the police. My children were told to keep off the grass. (There are no sidewalks.) My tree fell across someone's fence, and I was sued. I longed for my farm, my fields, where a weed in bloom is beauty and a bark is lost in the wind.

One Sunday soon after our arrival in Los Angeles I took on the real estate section of the *Los Angeles Times*, a newspaper which is a smorgasbord of information compiled to cater to the dreams and the curiosity of a city where recreation is compulsive and Jack need never worry about being a dull boy. There I found words and phrases offered up in tiny type which ignited me. "Ranches," "Country Property," "Acreage," "Ideal for Horses." Land in huge chunks from Idaho to Mexico was described in irresistible adjectives. Stables, corrals, trout streams, grazing rights all there among Puppies for Sale and Furnished Rooms. I felt like a man on Madison Avenue staring at a Tahiti poster. A dream had been born, and on Sunday after Sunday I turned to this tantalizing catalogue of freedom, reading every listing. Land was cheap in Oregon. Grass was scarce in Nevada. Real ranches lay "within minutes" of Los Angeles.

I did nothing about it for months. My job took up most of my time, and my first and second mortgages took most of my money. I found myself out there on Saturdays with the rest of my neighbors, manicuring my mat of Dicondra, washing my car, picking up the leaves which had had the audacity to settle for a moment on my property. Then a call came from Benny Goodman, who was playing at a place called Lake Tahoe. "You've got to see it," he told me, so off we went on our first western excursion. We drove up the center of California through the Mojave Desert, up along the Sierras and, finally, into the Carson Valley. There, between snow-capped peaks and barren foothills, lay a great, green oasis. Ranch houses nestled against the wall of the High Sierras, while miles of green stretched out across the valley. Cattle bent to graze, and cowboys rode right out of my television set to rustle the dust on country roads. I patted my trusty Thunderbird and rode on.

After an evening of Goodman and gambling, which I enjoyed because I play both clarinet and the odds, I was up and on my way to Carson City early next morning, heading for the nearest real estate office. Freddie and I located one next to the Capitol, across the street from the old Carson City Mint where Virginia City silver was turned into silver dollars, an arrow-shot from an old gambling hall and not more than a rifle-shot from a Paiute Indian reservation. At last I was in the West. If I had a six-shooter and there had been a chandelier in that office, I would have shot out the lights. Carson City, where Mark Twain almost fought a duel, where a convicted murderer once was elected attorney general, where men are men and women are blackjack dealers. My real estate salesman looked me up and down, but because my enthusiasm was obvious and my bank balance was not, I suppose he believed me when I told him I was interested in a small ranch. Off we drove in his car to the town of Genoa (accent on the "o"), four corners, four buildings, and, so far as I could see, four people, once the capital of Nevada and still fairly dripping with Old West.

Just down the road we turned into a long dirt driveway leading to what must have been a house or a resurrected mine shaft or a railroad track rolled up. Beyond the "building" one hundred sixty acres of deep green pasture, watered by melting snows from the mountains, stretched before me, sloping down from the driveway to a far-off fence line.

"The house needs a little work," the agent muttered.

"It looks a little like Eeyore's house," Freddie remarked. "After Pooh moved it, at that."

7

But I wasn't listening. All I could hear was water trickling down into an irrigation ditch in the lower field. All I could see was grass and horizon.

"How much?" I asked.

"They're asking five hundred an acre. You might get the whole thing for sixty-five thousand."

I thought of my Los Angeles house. I started off across the Carson Valley. I kicked a rock. "Let's make an offer," I almost whispered.

On the way back to Lake Tahoe Freddie had to ask what I thought I was doing. "It's four hundred and fifty miles from Los Angeles," she said. "Do you plan to commute?"

"It's a steal," I answered. "Where else can you find land like this for less than five hundred an acre with snow-capped mountains and gambling thrown in? What's a nine-hour drive when you own a ranch in the Carson Valley?"

"The only room with a roof is the kitchen," she continued.

"The value's in the land," I explained.

"So is most of the house."

We discussed it all the way home, but nothing could discourage me. I had made an offer on a ranch. I was almost a well-known Nevada rancher. Whitewashed fences already surrounding my spread, a saddle slung over a gate, a horse tied to a post near the main house. My herd grazed in the shadow of the Sierra. My hired man waited by my side for the roundup. The smell of saddle leather made my eyes water.

At the end of the following week my Carson City man called me. "We lost it," he told me. "A guy from Minden got it for sixty-eight. I guess he was just waiting for somebody else to make an offer."

But by that time I had come around to Freddie's opinion. The Carson Valley was among the most beautiful anywhere, I told myself, but it was too far away for my ranching plans unless I intended to live there, and even I had enough sense to know I wasn't ready to support myself and my family as a rancher. I accepted my defeat and went back to the Sunday *Times*.

8

After several months of studying, I became attuned to ranch listings. As my eyes scanned the columns, the word "ranch" would pop out at me all over the pages. But I was also becoming educated in the Southern California meaning of the word, one of the great distortions in modern real estatese. Everything here is called a ranch. Housing developments are ranches, individual lots are "suitable for ranches," and every long one-story house is a ranch. Where once large ranches had covered the area, tracts now have replaced them. Hundreds of bite-sized ranches lure us all. White board fences divide an acre into three or four lots, houses sprawl across them, and a horseshoe is nailed to a mailbox. A ranch is born. In more expensive areas a central stable is provided, and on weekends residents can ride around the tract, herding houses, not cattle, but still ranchers. It doesn't take a whiff of manure to call a house a ranch.

For the budget rancher there are smaller places called "ranchos." Spanish in Southern California is also a part of the real estate charisma. It is illegal in Los Angeles to build houses less than five feet apart, but still quite possible for next-door neighbors to shake hands or fists without leaving their own living rooms. It is also madness to build houses on expensive land more than five feet apart and not really ethical to call these ranches. So many are called ranchos. The owners think of themselves as rancheros, and nobody worries about it. Just don't attempt to wear a wide-brimmed sombrero, you gay rancheros. It would never fit between your ranchos.

There are also, by God, ranchettes. These are not small French ranches for girls, just small ranches or ranchos in no immediate danger from Indian raids, but always in peril of foreclosure by the nearest Savings and Loan. Finally, I discovered that ranches also come on wheels. For the restless rancher, I suppose. There are trailers, or more properly, "mobile homes" called variously "Ranch Home," "Ranch House," "Ranch Wagon," "Rancho," and even "Ranchero." Can you imagine a grizzled Jimmy Stewart beset by gun-slingers, prairie fires, and cattle rustlers, becoming discouraged by it all and simply towing his ranch away?

There are no farms in California, only ranches, judging by the ads. There are no ponds, only lakes. There are no brooks, only rivers. No matter that the ranches are often the size of taco stands, the lakes the size of puddles, and the rivers usually dry. The population explosion has made smallness a fact of life, but the Western dream lingers on. Any nobody would think of using the word *ranchito* to describe his spread.

The Carson Valley plunge happened in the first year of our California residence, and I continued on each succeeding trip to Lake Tahoe to look longingly at the ranches there. But aside from almost buying a small casino and mineral hot springs establishment (you could sit in a pool of steaming hot water, then rush off to the crap table) I made no more offers in Nevada. During the next four years, however, the ranch fever never left me, and wherever I went I visited ranches for sale. On a trip to Seattle I waded across Oregon fields in the rain, but decided against buying. We inspected eastern Washington - why I can't remember - and worked our way down to a ranch outside of Susanville, California, where again common sense and comments from agents like "If you fly your own plane, you're only a couple of hours from Los Angeles," stopped me.

I looked and talked and backed off. I was tempted on the outskirts of Las Vegas and again in Phoenix. North of San Diego looked promising for a while, and we once found ourselves inspecting, in a place called "Twenty-nine Palms," an old mansion surrounded by corrals and stables, a steal at one hundred forty thousand. It was clear by this time, even to me, that a ranch that was a ranch could not be bought within commuting distance of Los Angeles unless you were Gene Autry or Warner Brothers. On the other hand, to buy one more than two or three hours from the city would require an additional investment of an airplane. I couldn't quite see myself in goggles and silk scarf flying to work in a crop duster; even driving to the airport to meet someone makes me nervous. I narrowed my search to a radius of one hundred fifty miles and bought an old Navy Colt revolver to practice quick draws.

One day we stopped for lunch just south of San Luis Obispo, and there in a lump corral next to the restaurant were three water buffalo, looking as if they had just fought an unsuccessful battle with a cloud of moths. Jeremy and I went over the fence for a closer look, and while I hummed "Home on the Range," the smallest of the three moved toward us and snorted.

"Could we buy him?" Jeremy asked. It was a reasonable question considering that her sister Nicole now owned a kangaroo rat and Susie had a Lhasa Apso, not an Italian sports car but a small Tibetan dog trained to lie on his lama's feet, but because there are no lamas with cold feet in California, reduced to growling and scratching himself. And Freddie was looking for an otter for the pool.

"How much is that small buffalo?" I asked a man who was pitching hay over the fence around the corral. He look at me strangely, so I asked again.

"Now what would you do with a buffalo?"

"Oh, try to build up a herd, I guess," I told him.

"Starting with one buffalo?"

"We're in a hurry," I explained.

The buffalo man forked another load of hay. "They're not for sale, mister. But if you really want to buy a buffalo, there's a ranch down in the Santa Ynez Valley full of them. I hear they run some kind of stampede every year. Turn off at Solvang and ask somebody.

"Let's go there, Daddy," Jeremy said, her face alight. We walked back to the car to head south along the freeway. I knew we were not going to buy a buffalo. Even Jeremy knew we were not going to buy a buffalo. There are zoning laws in Los Angeles against buffalo. And they obviously attract moths. We drove down the freeway toward home and turned off at the sign for Solvang.

"A little buffalo wouldn't mind our backyard," Jeremy said.

We stopped at the first group of stores we came to in Solvang, a liquor store, a real estate office, and a bakery, representing, as I was to learn, three of the town's principal occupations. Freddie and the girls headed for the bakery, and I entered the real estate office.

A tall, bald man wearing cowboy boots, a shirt with pearl buttons, and a silver belt buckle introduced himself as Jim Farmer and asked what he could do for me.

"I was told they sold buffalo around here," I announced. "I don't really want one, but my daughter does."

Farmer hadn't expected that. "Well, there was quite a herd of them at a ranch near here. Used to get out now and then, but they're gone now. I doubt if there's a buffalo left in the Valley."

"What's this world coming to." I sighed.

"I can drive you out there and show you where they used to be," Farmer offered. "It's really quite a ranch. Quarter of a million in fences alone."

I accepted. I don't know yet why I wanted to go to a place where buffalo used to be, but I accepted. I rounded up the troops in the bakery and joined Farmer in his car for my first ride through the Santa Ynez Valley. As we drove out of Solvang into the gold and green, I brought up the subject of ranches. In fact, I came right out and asked if there were any small ranches for sale in the area.

"I'll show you one on the way," Farmer said. "People have to go to Oregon, so it's got to be sold."

Once again the old feeling stole over me. "How big?" I asked.

"It's three and a half acres, but you can probably pick up another three and a half with it. That'd give you a nice little spread."

"Has it got a house?" Freddie asked.

"The house is four years old," he told her. "Four bedrooms, three baths, and they just built a new stable with three stalls."

"Three horses!" Jeremy cried.

Farmer nodded and turned into a dirt road, past two houses and along a sweep of dry pasture to a low-roofed house almost obscured by evergreens. As we turned into the driveway, the comments began.

"It's a pretty house," Nicole announced.

"And a big lawn," said Susie.

From Jeremy, "They've got a pony."

We all got out while Farmer rang the bell and apologized to the owner, Mrs. Small, for arriving without warning, but she was proud of her house and her yard and willingly showed us both. Inside, the house was cool and dark on that sunny afternoon. A large, wood-paneled family room led off a country kitchen. An even larger living room with floor-to-ceiling fireplace stretched across the front of the house, and beyond lay sunny bedrooms and modern bathrooms. We walked through it all, whispering to each other our approval. Outside, the lawn and fringe of trees covered an acre, all beautifully tended, while just beyond the trees a small stable matching the house opened on a corral enclosed by cedar rails. We loved it all.

Farmer was busy explaining the wells and drainage, but I wasn't listening. I could see that Mrs. Small didn't want to sell the ranch, but it was for sale. It was a two-hour drive from Los Angeles, and no matter in which direction I faced I couldn't see another house. I gazed out for the first time across those fields I already felt I knew, while Farmer droned on about mean temperatures and future five-acre zoning. It was the first ranch I had ever seen in this valley, and it was all I wanted to see. I could hardly wait to make an offer.

We left Mrs. Small, who seemed to suspect that she had just lost her ranch, and drove off. "What's she asking?" I blurted out as soon as we were in the car.

"She wants fifty-five. Came down from fifty-eight. I'd offer her fifty-two. Then you can pick up that adjoining pasture for ten or eleven and you'll have a nice little place."

I turned to the back seat for approval, got it, and told Farmer to make an offer, providing he could pick up the piece from whoever owned it. We drove back to Solvang certain we had finally found my elusive ranch. Farmer drew up the offer while I sat in his office, overwhelmed. After I had signed it, made out a check for an amount I did not have in the bank, and thanked him, I rounded up the girls in the bakery again and off we went.

"I have a feeling we'll get it," I told them all.

"Which room is mine?" Nicole asked, then decided for herself.

"What happened to the buffalo?" Jeremy asked.

"Wait," I cried. "Wait till we get it. Then we'll have room for anything."

"Whoever would have thought," Susie said quietly, "that after looking for a ranch for five years we'd find one on a buffalo hunt."

2

*"Any ranch owner knows
that the two most important ingredients
for a successful cattle ranch
are water and grass."*
- CORNELIUS VANDERBILT, JR.

"You bought the Small ranch!"

The call came from Jim Farmer at the end of the following week. It was late in August, and there would be the usual sixty-day period of escrow, but Farmer had managed to put the two three-and-one-half acre pieces together into one big, beautiful seven-acre parcel of paradise. In the center of the Santa Ynez Valley, surrounded by pasture and fields of alfalfa, on a road of my own, it seemed as impressive to me as the Spanish ranchos of old California. I leaned back in my chair in my office in Hollywood and felt good.

During those sixty days I drove to the Valley several times to sign papers and talk to Farmer about my plans. I stayed away from the ranch, afraid, I suppose that the sight of me would change Mrs.

Small's mind, but I drove around the Valley, meeting people, admiring the seemingly endless miles of open fields and oak-shaded paths. Deer, driven from higher ground in search of water at the summer's end, lay in the shade of trees along the road. White-faced steers, keeping their own company, scowered dry pasture for what remained of spring grass, and horses, their chins resting on fences, dozed undisturbed. I looked forward to joining them all.

During this time the girls and I tried to name the Ranch. We discussed Flying Lazy Bar Triple T names without ever settling on any we liked, while Jim Farmer continued to introduce me to his friends as the new owner of the Small ranch. I am still known as "the fella who bought the Small ranch," and I suppose I always will be, although why their name could not have been King I don't know. Every time I have to call for help, which is every weekend, I am forced to identify myself as the new owner of the Small ranch. How long will it be before I can call a plumber and simply say, "This is Townsend over at the Big T. My faucet won't shut off"?

In the first weeks of ranching I decided to concentrate on the house itself, making it at least liveable for weekends. It was a wise decision, for it was the last time I was able to spend any money on furniture, but with heavy frosts at night and winter rains due at any time, there was little to do outside. I bought seven beds and a refrigerator and felt I was ready for anything. I could make ice cubes and lie down. But the rest of my family seemed to need something more, so I began to borrow old lamps, blankets, dishes, and towels. Soon it was possible to eat a meal at the ranch, read a book, and sleep. Then my friend Jim Farmer offered me a table with four chairs, and that completed my furnishings. Thoreau had one chair for solitude, two for friendship, and three for society. I did him one better by having a fourth for my feet, and I spent my first winter weekends reading on two chairs, anxious to begin the job of turning the Small ranch into a spread I'd be proud of. I decided to begin with grass.

On a Saturday morning in February of my first winter I sat with Jim Farmer in the Pancake House in Solvang and heard for the first time that what I needed for my field was "permanent pasture."

16

That sounded nice and substantial to me, and I agreed that that was just what I had been needing for a long time.

"You go over and talk to Anderson," Jim told me. "He'll disc your field and plant it while the ground's soft. Then a few more rains in March and April will start it off. After that, all you have to do is irrigate."

Farmer and his ranching friends have a way of making everything sound so simple, so inevitably successful as they sip their coffee on stools at the Pancake House. ("All you have to do is lay one-inch pipe below the frost line in your yard and hook it up to the main water outlet," one Marlboro cowboy advised me when I inquired about putting in a sprinkler system. Had he every laid one-inch pipe below the frost line? The damned trouble was, he probably had, and it had all worked beautifully.) All I had to do now was find Anderson and pay him to turn six acres of packed soil into six acres of permanent pasture. I left for his house in a hurry. That was the only rapid progress toward my new pasture that was made and I learned, as I have been learning every since, that time is not to be tampered with in that quiet valley. A mare should foal while spring grass is green and tender. Hay should be covered before the rains. Cattle should be sold before they cost too much to feed. Otherwise, a man's work must never interfere with his pleasure. The sun and the sunset will also come tomorrow. There is a leeway in life that only country people know, a time for leaning back, fingers tucked under the belt, and saying very slowly, "Well."

Mr. Anderson met me at this front door, and when I had identified myself as the new owner of the Small ranch, he agreed readily to my permanent pasture plans.

"I'll be down that way in a week," he said, and I had to let it go at that. But he wasn't. I watched for him the following week, and when it was clear that Mr. Anderson and his tractor were not going to arrive, I drove to his house and knocked on his door again. He was there, looking relaxed. "Still too wet," he explained to save me the trouble of asking him. "Maybe next week."

Two more sunny weeks went by while I waited for Mr. Anderson. But I was also waiting for an electrician to fix a live wire dangling from an outside light and a plumber to come back for the third time to allow me to turn on the bathtub water. Also, I was out of natural gas, and it was cold. I was so busy waiting that I didn't see Anderson's tractor until he was headed down the road to my house, trailing his discing equipment in a cloud of dust. I rushed out to meet him.

He shut off the ancient engine and climbed down. "Looks about right," he said, pointing to the field. "If it's too wet it just clogs everything up." Back he climbed and tilted his straw hat at a jauntier angle. "You ever found any arrowheads here?"

"I haven't looked for any," I told him.

"Well, you may find some today. I turn up lots of them discing. Why don't you just follow along and keep your eye out?"

A few arrowheads would be nice on the wall, I thought, so I followed him into the field and marched along behind as he drove up and down my six acres, turning up ground. My eyes were glued to the dark soil, but I saw nothing, not even a stone. And the walking was not easy, stumbling over the tilled ground behind Anderson's fuming machine. He stopped after a couple of trips to wipe his brow.

"See any?"

"Not one."

He shrugged and gunned the tractor again. Up and down we went, Anderson sitting comfortably on his perch while I stumbled along behind. It took him two hours to dig up my field. When he was finished, he drove his rig back onto the road and stopped to wave good-bye.

"I'll be back to seed next week. You buy the mixed seed at the mill, and I'll pick it up."

I said I would and watched him clatter off down the road. When I drove to Solvang to buy the hundred dollars' worth of seed the mill recommended, I stopped off to visit with Farmer.

"He have you out looking for arrowheads?" he asked.

"He did mention it," I admitted.

Farmer laughed. "Old Anderson's always looking for arrowheads. I don't suppose he's found one in five years."

18

It's a nice hobby, though, looking for arrowheads.

After a few weeks of ranching weekends another country problem arose. I was knee-deep in trash, and there were no collectors to haul it off for me. I don't know how the early pioneers solved the problem of rubbish on the Western plains. Perhaps they buried it, or perhaps they handled the problem the way Mark Twain's companions handled the distribution of mail along their stagecoach route to Nevada - they simply tossed it out as they went along. I could do neither on my ranch, and the enclosure beside my garage was piling up to the brim. I called for help and discovered the county dump.

Everybody in the Valley, it seemed, waited until he had a load, then drove to the dump once every week or two. At that time I was driving a new Cadillac with large trunk space, so one Saturday morning I loaded up with cans and boxes of accumulated debris and headed for the dump site behind the town of Solvang. It was not difficult to find, for halfway there I found myself following several pickups loaded with trash, and the parade wound through the hills to a final manmade mountain of cans and bottles. The keeper of the dump, who has long since become my friend and advisor, is a swarthy man in a tin hat who spends his days at the dump, and because, like the Pancake House and the small park in the center of town, it is one of the social centers of the Valley, he is one of the best informed men in the area. When I drove in that first morning, I had to wait in line while the dump keeper prowled the mountain of cans, obviously in search of something. At last he found it and returned to the gate to accept our fifty-cent entrance fee.

"Sorry to hold you up," he said with a grin when he got to me. "I needed a pen."

"Did you find one?"

"Oh, sure," He held up a battered ballpoint. "You can find anything you need here. I got a washing machine yesterday. Works fine too."

He showed me where to back into a heap of old boxes, and

there I deposited my first load of trash. As I pulled out again, the pickups were parked all around me, and whole families were discussing their affairs. Wives leaned out of truck cabs, children waved from truck beds, and the men stood in the shadow of the great trash pile talking. It was all so sociable that I didn't even mind the eye-watering fumes from the dump. I did, however, feel somewhat out of place in my Cadillac and resolved to buy a truck.

I've made dozens of trips to the dump since then and have become accepted, so to speak. Several of my Valley friends I see only on Saturday mornings. There is, after all, an inescapable intimacy that springs up among people who know each other's refuse that well. Bean cans, bourbon bottles, worn-out girdles, vintage vacuum cleaners tell more about a man's life than he would want to reveal to strangers.

Recently a new dimension has been added to the excitement of going to the dump. The County of Santa Barbara is required by law to provide a place to unload its citizen's waste material, but apparently there is no law requiring them to keep it in the same location, nor any commitment to notify us when they move it. The game we now play is, "Find the Dump," and, taken with patience and good nature, it need not lead to violence. But when you start off early on a Saturday morning with a full load of rotten hay, old barbed wire, and strong-smelling remnants from the kitchen, only to discover that the dump site is closed and moved across town, it does take a certain simple-minded good humor to resist the urge to leave the whole mess in the middle of the road. The dump we are using now, near the airport, is filling up. My friend in the tin hat shrugs when I ask him where it will be next week.

"They haven't told me," he says. "But we can't stay here. I found a phonograph this week, though, the kind you need cylinders for. People will throw anything away."

I left him at the gate. He leads an exciting life. Treasure. Travel. Ever-changing topography!

My field was seeded in late February, and my timing could not have been better if I had been shown a preview of nature's plans for March and April. For the rains came again, and my small pasture took part in the pageant our Valley enjoys between February and early May. It is a time when gardeners, nature's disciplinarians, whose horizon is only a hoe handle away, fight blisters and despair as the rising grass refuses to be stopped. But for most, who look across to the hills, it is a marvelous time when the Valley, puffed with pride, turns deep green. Field beyond field swells a foot or two with every plant which has been burned black to the roots for eight rainless months, and oat hay, wild mustard, burr clover, and rye grass mix harmoniously together. This sea of green is short-lived, however, and by June only scattered green patches, where men have chosen to irrigate, remain. Where the land must wait for rain, the emerald stalks turn to amber again, and only the roots remember.

While the ground was soft I decided to fence in my pasture. After all, if a blade of grass could so easily come up during that period, perhaps a fence post could go down, and if my ranch was to become the place I dreamed about, it would have to be enclosed. I began, naturally, with plans to extend the cedar posts and rails which already skirted the house, but a call to the lumber yard dismissed that idea. No cedar was available, and if it ever became available, it would be cheaper to go where cedars grow, chop them myself, and charter a railroad to carry them west. I then turned to white board fencing, that symbol of Southern California which distinguishes a house from a ranch. But to surround my pasture with painted boards would cost up to five thousand dollars, according to the estimates I was given, and I could not see myself explaining to my family that a white fence was more important than a pool in Los Angeles or a trip to Hawaii. I descended to the lowest common denominator, barbed wire and steel fence posts.

Once again I was educated at the Pancake House in the art of fence building. This time my ranching experts really enjoyed themselves, for it is an exhilarating experience for anyone who has ever put up a barbed-wire fence to sit down comfortably and tell somebody else how to do it. Jim Farmer came to the rescue by offering to help me set the six-by-four posts at key positions, leaving to me the "easy" job of putting in the steel posts. We bought all kinds of posts, rolls of wire, bags of staples, aluminum gates, hammers, and wire cutters. The pile in my garage looked high enough to divide the West into small squares.

Farmer arrived early one Saturday morning on his tractor, on the rear of which was a post-hole digger. We spent most of the day setting heavy wooden guideposts at corners and other intervals around the field, but with a power-driven bit to make the holes and an experienced rancher, which Farmer certainly is, to set the posts straight, the job seemed easy. I found myself doing what I do best - gesturing, holding a post straight while Farmer rooted it in the ground, walking behind the tractor looking for arrowheads, and resting. After the guideposts were in and the gates hung, Farmer gave me more tools and drove away, leaving me to complete the job. Because no one knows when he might have to string barbed wire, I'll be glad to explain the method. The fact that my fence had to be strung over again by somebody else need not make these instructions less credible.

The first rule of fencing is impossible to obey. It is most important to keep a straight line, not only for aesthetic reasons, but because the straighter the fence, the stronger it is. Reasonable, even if impossible. So I began by stretching string between the wooden guideposts. By setting the posts along the line of the string, there should be a correspondingly straight line of posts. (Are you paying attention, Cornelius Vanderbilt, Jr.?) I must say the string looked great, and if I had stopped right there it would have been a straight, if flimsy fence. My next step was to set the steel posts six feet apart along the string. There is a tool known to me variously as a fence-post-pounder-inner or a heart-attack-bringer-onner, depending upon whether you are looking at it or trying to use it. It consists of a long, cast iron bar, hollow at one end, with cross bars for handles, and it weighs fifty pounds when you begin to pound a post into the ground and two hundred pounds when you finish. The top of the post is placed in the hollow end, then with a mighty heave on the handles the post is set upright. After that, by lifting the pounder high in the air and bringing it down hard on top of the post, you drive the post gradually into the ground. Once the post has been sunk to the required depth, a vast upward heave lifts the pounder off the top of the post and back down hard upon your toe. All this, of course, must be done without touching the string, but always in perfect line with it.

For a beginner, it is wise to limit this exercise to, perhaps, a dozen posts a day. By that time the fence builder is purple with exhaustion and the pounder-inner too heavy to lift. So, leaving the string, the posts, the pounder, and the Band-Aids in the grass, I went back inside the ranch house and went to bed. But I was back at it again the following Saturday morning, and another dozen red-and-white posts were beaten into the ground. I continued in this fashion along the entire southern side of my field, perhaps a thousand feet, and before I stopped to admire my work I was blistered and sore. My line of posts was not quite straight. In fact, if it is true, as I have been told, that cattle follow a fence line, mine would be dizzy by the time they walked from one end of the field to the other. But I was not about to begin again, so I rolled out the reel of barbed wire.

Barbed wire is "tricky," as some Western wag has written. But three strands of it had to be strung along my fence line, anchored to corner posts, stretched tight, and fastened to each steel post along the way. Wearing heavy gloves helps, but actually a complete suit of armor wouldn't protect anyone against barbed wire because it is alive and has a vicious, vindictive mind of its own. It snaps back, wraps itself around your ankles, and does not yield to rage or reason. I began all right, twisting one end of the first strand firmly around a wooden post and stapling it securely. But stretching it, even with wire stretchers, keeping it taught while I fastened it to the next post, always aware that it would spring back at me at will, proved to be impossible. I worked all morning on one strand and gave up. Whoever fenced the West, no matter how he may have loused up grazing rights, has my admiration.

I hate to write here that I slunk back to the Pancake House, so I'll say simply that I obtained help through certain sympathetic friends. My savior was a man named Magnus Jepson, a wonderful, pink-faced Scandinavian in his sixties who looks like Santa Claus on a Western vacation. And he has only one arm; the other, severed at the elbow, has been replaced with an ingenious device, like a pair of pliers, controlled by pulleys. Magnus, a name he richly deserves, took a look at my fence and, with a jolly, twinkling grin, observed that it was a little crooked.

"Does it really matter?" I asked somewhat testily. "I don't mind it myself."

"Oh, yes," he assured me. "It's got to be straight. I better see what I can do."

I left him. I didn't want to watch him tear our my posts, ho ho ho, and set them all straight. I didn't want to watch him pound posts back in again with one hand. In fact, I didn't want a fence at all. But Magnus Jepson, bless his merry soul, reappeared a few hours later to ask for my help with the barbed wire.

"I'll stretch it while you fasten it to the posts," he suggested.

Hah! He couldn't do it alone either. I hurried out with him to see a line of posts set as straight as an arrow and barbed wire unwound and ready in the grass. With a claw hammer in his real hand and barbed wire held in his mechanical hand he stretched the wire tight across the posts, while I wound fasteners around it. And in a single afternoon we had completed one whole side of the pasture fence.

"I've done a mile a day of fencing," Magnus told me when we stopped, "but that was before I lost my hand."

I felt like challenging him to a clarinet duo, but I resisted. Be kind to the handicapped, I always say.

In May I climbed to the roof of my house to install a weather vane. It is a golden horse prancing on an arrow, and, like my original fence, it is not quite straight. An afternoon breeze sweeps across the Valley all summer, arriving at noon each day, leaving quietly just before sunset. My golden horse resists this breeze, never moving at all, headed always and confidently westward. I like the weather vane, though, and admire its resistance to the whims of the wind. There is something decisive about a motionless weather vane.

But the persistent breeze skimmed off the moisture from the land, and fountains of water appeared throughout the Valley wherever growth must continue. It was time, as my ranching friends had predicted, to irrigate. I called a pipe company in Santa Maria and arranged to rent the equipment to keep my pasture permanent. Fenced, knee-deep in grass and assorted weeds, it was almost ready, even if I was not, to support a herd or a flock or a bunch of something, but I had been advised to give it a summer of growth and water before putting animals on it.

My pipes arrived on Saturday, as most things must because it is my only full day at the ranch, and were unloaded and carried through my new gate at the far end of the field. First came the four-inch aluminum pipes in thirty-foot intervals. This, my pipe man told me, would handle the whole job. He set them up for me, attached the line to an outlet from our community well, and turned them on. Twenty geysers rose simultaneously from the deep grass, great plumes of spray, each jerkily turning to cover a full sixty-foot circle with water. My irrigation had begun.

I think I have come to know this collection of pipes better than anything else at my ranch. Not that they are particularly worth knowing, for, like every other foolproof invention, there is always the fool against whom they are not proof, but because I spend an hour or two every ranching day with my pipes. They are moveable, which means that I move them, one at a time, up and down my pasture, hooking them together late in the afternoon, running water through them all night, then unhooking them the next morning and moving the whole system sixty feet to the next parched area. For thirty-foot tubes of aluminum they are light in weight, but before I pick up pipe number twenty they seem heavier. They are made so that they fit together as easily as freight cars are coupled, but on bad days they don't fit together at all. The rainbirds, rising on foot-long stems at the end of each pipe, are also foolproof; that is, until all twenty are lined up across the field and the water is turned on. Then every other rainbird refuses to rain. My next move is to start down the line again, getting slapped in the face by

25

the gushers from the rainbirds that do work, while I poke the end of a coat hanger down the ones that are plugged up. Sometimes this works. Sometimes nothing does.

Hauling pipes is one of the things I really do well. In ankle-deep mud, tall grass, blistering heat, I march on, dragging my pipes down the field, hunting for the one I just moved, then hooking onto it. It does sometimes seem a long way from shoot-outs and trail drives, especially when I stumble home covered with mud, my shoes filled with burrs, dripping water from the tip of my nose. But perhaps this is a side of the West we don't see on television. And it sustains me to know that nobody anywhere can move those pipes better than I. It is also fulfilling to drive along my road at twilight, clean again, and to see the twenty water spouts rising from the grass like twenty whales in a grassy sea and to know I put them there. But it is a responsibility too. All that grass depending on me, needing me, knowing I'll be there.

In early April I made my annual trip to Phoenix to spend a day with my accountant. I was braced to tell him about the ranch, an indulgence he would no more understand than I understood him, but after twenty years of being right, at least in his addition, he deserved to know. Lou began and still belongs in Brooklyn, where he feels at home. In the early fifties he took what for him was the equivalent of the Lewis and Clark Expedition by moving to Manhattan. By then he owned several Brooklyn properties to fall back on, as well as two Manhattan apartment buildings, and, while he was uneasy that far west, he did own the building. If a tenant did not like his accent, Lou would simply raise the rent. If it took courage for my accountant to venture out of Brooklyn, it took sheer panic to send him to Phoenix. Ten years ago he moved to a house in that well-baked community to escape The Bomb. Deserting lower Fifth Avenue and the Catskills, he settled for a grove of grapefruit trees, convinced that Phoenix would either escape entirely or be the last place to blow up.

In recent years Lou has changed his habits. Now he spends three winter months in Manhattan and three summer months at the

Concord. Knowing him as well as I do, I am certain that this compromise was reached only through top secret information. Somehow he has learned that The Bomb will not be dropped on New York in winter or summer. In fall and spring he is safe in Phoenix. I know that when the rest of the world is rubble, my friend Lou will still be taking depreciation, perhaps somewhat accelerated. Secure in that knowledge, I trust him completely to prepare my taxes.

"I've bought a small ranch two hours from Los Angeles," I said while he sharpened pencils, like a dentist preparing his drill.

"A farm, you mean?"

"No, a ranch."

"We'll call it a farm. Tell me, what can you get for it?"

"I paid sixty-two-five," I told him. "But I don't want to sell it."

"Would you take ninety? Put it on sale for ninety thousand dollars."

"Nobody will pay that for it, Lou."

"Then we won't sell it." He began now to add up figures on a long yellow pad, blowing little puffs of air through his nose, which he does just before he tells a joke.

But I know all his jokes. "I'm interested in deductions," I interrupt him.

"What's going on there?" he asked, already laughing at this joke.

"Trees and permanent pasture."

"Walnuts?" he asked excitedly. "Very deductible, walnuts."

"No walnuts."

"You sure?" He was making little circles on the pad which might have been walnuts. "How do you know you don't have walnuts? After all, I didn't know I had grapefruit. Look around for some little things hanging down from the trees. They might be walnuts."

"There are no little things hanging from my trees, Lou."

"What do people raise there?" More puffs of air came from his nose.

27

"Mostly race horses," I told him. "And livestock."

"Sheep are nice," he said, beginning to draw a sheep.

"Not on my spread," I assured him, remembering what sheep had done to destroy the West for cattle.

"Then try some cows."

"Steers," I corrected.

"So steers."

It was settled. Now I could buy my herd, while Lou took depreciation on them or drew their pictures on a tax form. I mosied out of his office to the elevator. I'm not bow-legged. As a matter of fact, I'm a little knock-kneed, but already I had that faraway look in my eye as grazing Angus dotted the parking lot.

"Get along," I cried as I started my car. I think I heard it moo a little.

3

*"Most anthropologists seem to agree
that there is absolutely no evidence
that the human mind, as such, has improved at all during
the last five hundred thousand years."*
- JOSEPH WOOD KRUTCH

In the town of Solvang there is a sightseeing bus built to look like an old trolley, with a large "69" painted on the front. At no charge the driver takes tourists around the town, pointing out examples of Danish architectural ingenuity, the Spanish-Mexican influence cropping up here and there in whitewashed adobe and red tile, and the familiar American contribution, service stations. The only thing we missed on our tour was a Gothic cement plant at one end of town and a trailer park on the other.

Even though I lived in comparative and very welcome isolation on my small ranch, I was already being affected by the social history of the Valley. Its architecture gave me my first clue.

Not being a geologist, with his layers of history stratified and spread before him like a petrified club sandwich, I made use of people and their documents to discover who and what were here before me. And I've decided to prepare and anthropological sandwich - a peopleburger - to describe the dwellers who preceded me in the Santa Ynez Valley. By stacking one of each variety on top of the other, beginning with prerecorded history and ending with a specimen I saw this afternoon, I offer my present and past neighbors. It makes a motley pile.

At the bottom of my sandwich is an all but squashed lump of black feathers with a pink, bald head sticking out, gasping what seems to be its last breath. This is the California condor, which, for the moment, owns more acreage than almost anyone else in the Valley. This largest of North American birds lingers near extinction on a government preserve along the east slopes of the mountains which separate our Valley and Santa Barbara, and is no match for anyone who has moved there since he arrived. There are, according to people who think they can count condors, about three dozen of these huge birds left, but only Jim Farmer, of all my acquaintances, has seen one, and his account of a condor take-off holds little hope for their survival. It seems the great bird has to run along the ground, flapping its wings like one of those pioneers of aviation in old newsreels, wings glued to his shoulders, who runs and flaps until he collapses in a heap of heart failure. The condor does get off the ground, but any bird that has made no more aeronautical progress than that in hundreds of thousands of years since Condor and Mammoth posed for those pictures in history books can't last long. A few grumbling ranchers wonder why a few dumb birds control more of the Valley than they do, but otherwise the condor is ignored. His family background is impressive, however, and he belongs at the bottom of my sandwich.

I will arbitrarily skip over the other nonhuman inhabitants of the Valley because, with few exceptions, they have been eliminated as hopeless pagans by missionaries or as dangerous threats by soldiers and hunters whose obligations it is to bury as much of nature as possible in order that future generations of the curious can devote careers to digging up what once was alive. The grizzlies and the mountain lions are gone from our hills, the eagles are gone from our skies, and what small animal life remains does so by virtue of the fact that it is too small to rope or too tough to chew.

Mashed down upon the condor, also breathing heavily from the weight of the more civilized pile on top of him, is a Chumash Indian, painted bright colors and no doubt holding his nose. Not, I must emphasize, because the condor has body odor (although, being a scavenger, he must have bad breath), but because the man on top of him, a missionary, hasn't washed since he was baptized. The Chumash and his ancestors have been living in the Valley for a thousand years or more, although the last full-blooded member of his tribe died in 1952. Because the Chumash tribe was known for gentleness, generosity, and cleanliness and because it made the fatal mistake of expecting in return these same Christian virtues from its white brothers, the Chumash and the condor population are now about equal. It remains to be seen which will outlast the other, but I am betting on the condor. After all, we are finally trying to save him, not his soul.

On the easterly foothills of the Valley is a magnificent lake, forty miles around, named Lake Cachuma, a Chumash word. Among the many things I am not is an etymologist, yet I devised a theory about how this lake got its name, and nobody at the Pancake House has contradicted me. The Chumash were great ones for building steam rooms, large underground houses where they would sit among the hot rocks, allowing the sweat to pour off them. When they were sufficiently dehydrated, they would all rush out and jump into very cold water. My theory holds that a couple of missionaries witnessed this ritual one morning on the shores of the lake, and when a band of Chumash emerged shivering from the water, they were all sneezing. The missionaries, unable to recognize a sneeze when it came out of an Indian, believed that the Chumash were trying to tell them the name of the lake. And so Lake Cachuma got its name. The fact that it is a manmade lake won't shake me out of believing this bit of folklore. I've made up my mind.

California's first successful chain of businesses was a series of twenty-one missions established by the Spanish and stretching up the coast; a necklace of Christian islands in a barbarous sea. The Mission Santa Ines was founded in 1804, and my missionary immediately began his zealous task of converting the heathen Chumash. His methods were so effective that in a mere thirty-five years there were hardly any Chumash left. In return for free labor by the Indians, which for a time made the Mission very successful, the missionary offered the Chumash lessons in Christianity, lodging in the mission compound, and all the exciting Caucasian diseases an Indian could catch. Under our missionary the average Chumash's life span was six years. How many Chumash souls were saved no one can say, but the missionary became the Valley's first owner of cattle and horses, and, unlike his Indian charges, he seemed to have survived nicely. Our Mission still functions today at the edge of the town, its white walls and red tile roof still sound, its bells solemn, joyous, startling.

Above the missionary in our social sandwich is, of all things, a rancher. And what a rancher he is, for his spread makes Lorne Greene's *Ponderosa* look like my field. The famous Spanish land grants divided up the Santa Ynez Valley into huge chunks and bestowed them on anyone in current political favor with the Mexican government. Mexicans, Americans who renounced their American citizenship for Mexican, and immigrants who happened to marry into the right family at the right time wound up with ranches the size of cities and set about raising cattle on a scale so large that it took days to find herds. That's what I call ranching! And from these great ranchos hundreds of square miles in size, through years of forced sales of land too expensive to keep, we have come down to mix six acres of permanent pasture. That's what I call subdivision!

The rancher, unlike the Indian, has survived, often on a grand scale, and our Valley society includes today men who can ride all day across their own land. His economy, however, has changed. Instead of selling ten thousand head of stringy cattle for two dollars apiece, he raises thoroughbred horses and sells their offspring for ten thousand dollars apiece, with tax write-offs thrown in. On the western edge of Solvang, for instance, is a ranch called *Flag Is Up Farms*. Jeremy and I visited it not long ago and watched in wonder as horses were exercised on a private race track, groomed in a stable that would make a Bel-Air mansion seem cramped, examined in a private horse hospital. As we walked around this testimonial to what horses can earn and men can spend, a man rode down from the main house to greet us on a very aristocratic horse.

"You're welcome to look around," he told us.

Jeremy walked toward his horse, and I knew what was coming. "Do you sell any of your horses?" she asked.

"Oh, yes," he said smiling. "We buy and sell."

"Is this one for sale?"

The man reined the horse toward her. "We just paid seven hundred and fifty thousand for this one."

Jeremy patted the horse's nose. "He's nice," she said, "but I guess we'd rather look for something less expensive."

The man rode on, and we walked off. I made up my mind then to find a horse for her, but perhaps not here at a ranch so exclusive it was called a farm. After all, the velvet nose and gentle eyes that bring together a little girl and a horse are also soft, also trusting at lower prices. Jeremy thought so too.

Above the rancher in my sandwich is a man colorfully costumed as the Chumash but far less vulnerable to the outside influences, even the social upheavals of our own century than any Indian ever was. He is a Dane, a thrifty, self-contained, hard-working man who is ready to smile but not to speak before he thinks about what he is going to say. He has lived in the Valley now for nearly sixty years, has founded and built a town still so much his own that Americans of other national origins, even those who have lived here longer than he has, often feel like foreigners in their own community. In fact, so strong has the Danish influence in the Valley surrounding Solvang become that most of us know more of the language, the customs, the food, and the architecture of Denmark than we could possibly need to know. Here in a remote valley in southern California, where for centuries Spanish, Mexican, and pioneer American families have lived together to build an economy based upon cattle, horses, and truck farming, the Danish pastry has suddenly taken over. The biggest holiday of the year is not July Fourth or even Christmas, but a weekend in September called Danish Days. Danish flags fly, Danish sausage sizzles, Danish skirts whirl.

It all began when a couple of Danish-Americans chose the sunny surroundings of the Mission Santa Ines to found a Danish folk school, but the first bakery was not far behind. Windmills soon followed, and before the ranchers knew what was happening, they were buying cattle troughs and cowboy boots, gopher pellets and pickup trucks from Danish merchants. Instead of steak and refried beans they were tasting Danish meatballs and raw fish. And to their consternation they discovered that there is more profit in cookies than cattle.

Solvang is today the center for most of the formal social life in our Valley. Roofing parties and folk dancing have replaced rodeos. My dream of sauntering into a general store, saying "Howdy," and ordering a few salt blocks and bacon sides has been shattered by the necessary alternative of entering a Danish market, mumbling "Go'da'," and settling for a half-dozen Danish apple crescents. What is the West coming to?

The thriving Danish community has attracted tradesmen and businessmen of other nationalities, and so long as they conform to the concept of "Little Denmark" they were welcome, and they also do well. But they are neither socially nor numerically important enough to belong in my sociological heap. There is one last layer who is, however, for he, instead of steers and thoroughbreds, is now the Valley's principal industry. On top of the Dane is the California tourist, dressed in an Aloha shirt, camera hanging from his neck, who arrives early each weekend to buy. The Valley population shrinks from his invasion, while the Danish shopkeepers court him, and he leaves late Sunday afternoon, clutching souvenirs, munching pastry, filled with admiration and aquavit.

That is my Santa Ynez sandwich. Five layers, five invasions, each removing something of the seemingly timeless beauty the conquerors came to enjoy. Perhaps only the condor is innocent, for his fare is carrion. To each of the others what lived must die, and survival is selfish. No wonder the eye of the steer is wary, the step of the deer is delicate. The Chumash, who love to bathe, lack water. The rancher who pins a calf to the ground gives up to the tax collector. Even the determined Dane cannot long withstand Colonel Sanders. Man replaced when he should replenish, and for cash he carries a valley away in the trunk of his car.

Soon after we moved into the ranch my daughter Susie fell at home in Los Angeles, breaking both hips. This put an end to weekend visits by Freddie and Susie. Nicole had just slipped past the magic age when horses, stray cats, and saddle shops are more fun than Saturday movies, so my ranch family was reduced to me and Jeremy. Jeremy and I and my new collie, Fernando, who had replaced Amber in my continuing succession of these gentle dogs, took on the ranch together, missing the others but discovering for ourselves that we could manage. Jeremy became the cook. Fernando took on the responsibility for chasing chickens out of the yard, stirring up the neighbor's dogs, and warning us of approaching plumbers. And I, of course, was the foreman, giving lots of orders to myself and carrying them out as well as I could. There was an unspoken bond of contentment between us, and long before we met anyone else in the Valley we knew that this was where each of us wanted to be.

My first meeting with our nearest neighbors precipitated what might be called The Great Battle of the Refugio Water Company, a skirmish fought without a shot fired over a plate of Danish cookies. Hardly the range war Barbara Stanwyck might have waged single-handed against a hangin' posse, but nevertheless crackling with possibilities. Among the mountain of papers Jim Farmer had asked me to sign when I bought the ranch I remember a document which made me a member of the Water Company, whose assets consisted of a community well and electric pump supplying water to seven property owners. I owned seven shares, one for each acre, in this enterprise, and for the right to use the water

I had agreed to pay six dollars per month per acre for what was referred to in the document as "Standby Water Rights."

The money was used to pay for repairs and other charges, and an annual meeting of stockholders was held in the living room of my nearest neighbor, a sturdy woman named Mrs. Petersen. Her husband, a good-natured Swede, operated a ham radio station and spoke most of the evening with other operators around the world. The reason I know this is that his conversations came in loud and garbled through the speakers of my phonograph. In the quiet passages of Ives or Sinatra records I often hear long conversations between Petersen and Saigon or San Diego.

I had yet to meet the other owners of the Water Company, but I did know that there was a family at the end of the road named de Vecchio with numerous children and a pony. (Jeremy immediately discovered its name and the fact that it was for sale.) A retired colonel named Pomfit rented a house next to the di Vecchios. I had not met anyone else until the battle began.

> An emergency meeting of the shareholders
> of the Refugio Water Company will be held
> at the home of Mrs. Petersen at 11:00 A.M.
> Saturday, June 11. Please attend.

An emergency! Had the well run dry? Were we being swallowed up by a conglomerate? I rushed to the Petersens' a few minutes before eleven, covered with mud from my pipe moving, ready for the crisis.

In the Petersens' living room, sipping coffee, sat seven people. Mrs. Petersen looked very businesslike, holding a file of papers on her lap. Mr. Petersen sat next to her, smiling without permission. To his right on the couch were the di Vecchios, he with a pipe, she with cigarette. Across the room Colonel Pomfit introduced himself, squeezing my hand until our knuckles cracked, while his wife nodded and continued to knit what looked like a windsock, a long, orange tube with holes at both ends. In a corner by himself was a completely bald man named Dingle who, it was

36

explained, owned three and one-half acres of brush between the Petersen and di Vecchio properties. I sat down.

Mrs. Petersen opened the meeting. "You are using standby water to irrigate your field," she told me.

"From four-inch pipes," added di Vecchio.

"Two-inch pipes," I corrected.

"Actually," Colonel Pomfit interrupted, "the main line is four-inch. The cross lines are two-inch."

"I've been carrying pails of water from the pony trough to wash my hair," put in Mrs. di Vecchio, an attractive brunette.

Mr. Dingle sipped his coffee thoughtfully. "I don't use any water," he told us.

"You don't need to wash your hair." Pomfit laughed to relax the mounting tension. Dingle gave him a sour glance.

"But I put in permanent pasture," I explained. "I have to irrigate it."

"It's standby water," Mrs. Petersen reminded me.

"And now it's shooting up in the air," di Vecchio added.

"But it's coming down again," I said.

Colonel Pomfit held out both hands like a second-base umpire. "The question here is whether we can allow standby water to shoot up in the air through four-inch pipes."

"Two-inch," I corrected.

Pomfit stood up. "Let's put it to vote."

"You can't vote," Mrs. Petersen reminded him. "You only rent."

I was seething. "What are we paying standby fees for if we can't use the water?"

"It's for reserve," they all said at once.

Then di Vecchio turned to me. "The well can't stand the pressure. We can only use water for our houses and lawns. You're taking it all."

I could see that no more sense was to come of this meeting. After all my work I was not about to see my six acres of pasture wither to brush like Dingle's field, but discussion was useless. "All right," I agreed, "let's vote."

"Somebody make a motion," Dingle suggested, wiping his head.

There was a flutter of whispers among my neighbors until finally Mrs. Petersen cleared her throat of cookie crumbs. "I move that no standby water be allowed to be used for irrigation."

"Second," put in di Vecchio.

"All in favor raise your hands."

Seven hands went up.

"You can't vote. You only rent." I reminded Pomfit and his wife, who had her hand raised through the orange windsock. Pomfit sat down, wheezing at my insubordination.

Mrs. Petersen counted hands. "Five people owning six and a half acres vote yes."

"And I own seven acres, and I vote no," I announced.

"He wins by half an acre," Dingle said.

"He'll blow out the pump," di Vecchio moaned.

"I'll cancel my lease," Pomfit decided.

"I'm glad I don't live here," Dingle whispered to me.

The meeting adjourned with glares. Each shareholder marched out the Petersens' side door shaking his head and mumbling. I went back to my pipes, but I didn't turn them on. It didn't seem to be the right moment.

I am not a man who savors victory at anyone's expense. In fact, I may be too sensitive for the West. I slow down at signs for Deer Crossings. I get headaches from Western hats. And I always have to go to the bathroom at the feed store, where they don't have one. As I say, I may not be cut out for nature's intention that the fittest survive. At any rate, having won, I conceded the victory and made arrangements with the Santa Ynez Water Conservation District to connect my pipes to the main water line. At considerably more cost to me, their water shoots out of my rainbirds, and Mrs. di Vecchio is no longer carrying pails from the pony trough. Colonel Pomfit saluted me the other day as he rode by on his horse. Even old Dingle offered to sell his brush to me. And I won another victory. I no longer pay for standby water, and Mrs. Petersen just left a large bag of peaches at my door.

In the first week of May I was invited to be the guest of the Rancheros Visitadores on their annual ride through the Santa Ynez Mountains. Well, I was not going to ride with them, and two days was all the time I could spend with the most exclusive, certainly the most famous group of riders in the West, but for a man who did not own a horse, who had yet to buy his first pair of Western boots, to be invited to join the five hundred Rancheros was an honor. I liked to think of it as an expression of confidence in my potential on the part of my two Pancake House sponsors, Jim Farmer and Ed McCarty, a builder of Valley houses who can carry a bale of hay on each shoulder.

The Rancheros Visitadores were established in 1930 as the modern version of the ride of the visiting ranchers after spring roundup between the missions of Santa Barbara and Santa Ines. In those days, when Mexico belonged to California, the ranchers would stop at each of the great ranches for as much hospitality as they could drink. The modern Rancheros decided to skip the visiting part, however, and to carry along in trunks their own hospitality, which awaited them at each of their campsites. The Rancheros are divided into fourteen camps of thirty to seventy members each, two or three hundred "Mavericks," or newcomers, who ride along for four or five years waiting to become full members as old Rancheros die, and another two hundred wranglers and bartenders. Mounted on their best horses, silver bridles polished, saddle bags filled with beer, they are an impressive sight at the start of their week-long trek. "Those seven wonderful days of comraderie, zestful, outdoor living, and warm festivity" were to begin the first Saturday in May. I polished my belt buckle, practiced drinking, and prepared to join them.

The ride of the Rancheros begins at the Jackson camp just outside of Solvang, when all who can climb aboard a horse or mule set out for the Mission, riding in a mile-long column across the spring-green fields once tilled by Mission Indians. Outside the Mission the riders sit on restless mounts, some waving to wives and children, some trying to remember from the previous year how to light a pipe, hold a hat on, and rein a horse with only two hands.

While the Rancheros band plays "The Lord's Prayer," the names of fellow Rancheros who have passed away during the year are read solemnly to a riderless horse, after which the Mission padre blesses the riders, then the wonderful creak of saddle leather, the jingle of spurs begin as the now silent riders turn back to their camp. The ride of the Rancheros is on, the fourteen camp bars are open, and nobody has fallen off a horse yet.

In the foothills east of Lake Cachuma where the rocky road of the Santa Ynez River winds down from higher elevations to circle a live-oak grove the main camp of the Rancheros Visitadores is permanently established. With my gate pass clutched in my hand I drove into the camp parking lot and was approved for the day by a guard who looked as if he had just robbed the morning stage at Los Olivos.

"How's the stock market this morning?" he asked me.

"Down," I told him.

"Park over there between those horse trailers."

It was official. I was an approved guest. This exclusive camp, where no stallions or women are allowed, where mares in heat must wear red ribbons around their tails, welcomed me and drove me in an old army bus to the camp headquarters. There I registered and set off to find Jim Farmer's camp, Los Vaqueros. Like the rest of the camps which circled the headquarters trailer and permanent mess hall, Jim's camp consisted of a large oak-log fire with a semicircle of two-man tents on one side, a bar and a trailer or two on the other, and a line of horses nuzzling hay just beyond the bar. My arrival, perfectly timed, caught the camp members on their way between a tiger-milk party which had begun at sunrise and the morning horse show, about to begin in a dusty arena near the camp. A few Rancheros hiccupped by the fire.

"Where can I find Jim Farmer?" I asked the groggy group.

"Over to the show," one said. "Follow the noise of the generator, turn right at the showers, and you'll hear the show."

After a short walk in the right direction I discovered another reason the Rancheros bar women and studs from their camp. On a platform at the side of the fenced arena a tall Ranchero was bellowing jovial insults, salted with language never before amplified, at the crowd. There is something apparently "warm and zestful" about a four-letter word that can be heard for half a mile.

I found Jim Farmer sitting in the grandstand next to a sleeping dog and Ed McCarty. Ed, smoking a pipe that looked like a burning stump, was enjoying the language, but my friend Jim, I could see, was uncomfortable.

"Cracked two ribs yesterday," he told me. "I was just sitting on my horse opening a bottle of Seven-Up when the damn thing squirted up in the air and spooked my horse. Threw me right off."

"Shoulda been drinkin' Scotch," Ed commented. The dog sighed.

We watched as the horse show got under way. The first contest was one in which each rider had to approach three barrels at full gallop, rein the horse around the barrels, and dash back to the finish line. It does not seem to be much of a challenge for grown men and grown horses, but, as I watched, I decided that I could never do it. I settled back against the sleeping dog and applauded the winner. The next event was a steer-roping contest in which two cowboys take off after at terrified steer, trying, before the steer reaches the end of the arena, to rope him fore and aft. I noticed one convincing rider who seemed to prefer to remain aloof from this dusty business, yet who obviously was known and admired by the audience. His name, I discovered, was Monty Montana, a familiar name to Western movie fans, a popular Ranchero here in the camp. I felt sure that old Monty was waiting for a greater challenge, and, sure enough, a steer broke out of the corral and headed pell-mell for the tents and bars of the camps. Monty whirled his horse and took off after the steer, roping him neatly and dragging him back just before he plunged into a cocktail party. The crowd roared its approval and Monty waved.

We walked back, Jim and Ed and I, to the Vaqueros clearing for a beer before lunch to find a tall cowboy sitting by the fire playing his guitar, across the neck of which was written "Peso Dollar" in mother-of-pearl. And that was his name. (Nobody who prints his name in mother-of-pearl on his guitar is ever named

41

Irving.) I sat next to this Rancheros minstrel and listened to the Western songs he sang, the dying fire at my feet, a cold can of beer in my hands, the dust of a roping contest on my shoes. As Peso sang, I decided he looked more like a Marlboro cowboy than any living man. His face was long and tanned, his hands, curled around guitar the strings, were shaped for a six-gun.

"You look more like a cowboy than any cowboy I ever saw," I told him.

"I know it," he answered in a perfect Southwestern accent. "Somebody's always asking me to ride the meanest horse around here because of they way I look." He strummed thoughtfully. "Actually, I work for the highway patrol in Globe, Arizona, and I just like to sing."

Then I'll be damned if he didn't shake out a Marlboro from a pack in his shirt pocket and offer me one. I accepted, sipped my beer, and asked him to sing, "El Paso." It was time for lunch.

The Rancheros were lined up with their stainless-steel trays outside the mess hall. We joined them and passed along steaming tables piled with steak and beans and pie, carrying our loaded trays to the long benches under a corrugated roof where we ate our lunch. At that moment I would rather have been eating lunch there in the noon dust of the Rancheros' camp than at any starched white table in any Oak Room in the world.

Later in the afternoon I met the world's greatest cowboy. Actually I saw him ride by on his way to a cutting contest in a corral behind the arena. Jim Farmer and I were standing under a live oak watching a semicircle of cowboys facing a semicircle of steers, each eyeing the other with some misgiving, when a tall young man rode past us.

"That's the greatest cowboy in the world," Farmer told me.

"How do you know?" I asked.

"He's won every rodeo prize there is," Jim explained. "Oh, he's the greatest cowboy in the world, all right."

"Didn't he lose last year to a girl up north somewhere?" Ed McCarty asked.

Farmer shook his head sadly. "Yes, I guess he did that once.

It happens now and then."

The greatest cowboy in the world beaten by a girl! It was like hearing that Jesse James had been outdrawn by his mother. My fallen idol rode past us again, but he did not seem quite so impressive to me. In fact, I thought he looked a little puffy.

The final event of the afternoon was a polo match played with several large red-and-yellow beach balls and with as much competitive spirit as a game of catch. Jim Farmer and I walked right through the center of this match without ever disturbing the players and headed for the Rancheros' noblest hour, the cocktail hour. At five each afternoon the fourteen camps renew themselves with fourteen cocktail parties, open to all members of all camps, each attempting to outdo the others in mountain hospitality. Rancheros, some showered and dressed in clean shirts, warm jackets, and Western hats sparkling with gold pins from their rides, some unshaven and bleary from the morning's tiger-milk binge, stroll from camp to camp, sampling what are laughingly called hors d'oeuvres. I was offered chunks of wild boar, buffalo, antelope, elk, and, of course, beef. Paper plates piled with these delicacies were thrust as us wherever we visited until we could hold no more and sank into chairs by our fire, where more drinks were served as the great mess-hall dinner bell rang. "Chow time," some clown announced, and off we went to dinner.

I cannot describe the dinner served by the Rancheros Visitadores. I am still to full to think about it, except that I remember my friend Peso Dollar sang to us and that the setting sun, which had tried in vain at lunch to penetrate the corrugated canopy above our heads, finally found us by sinking low enough to shine through the open sides of the mess hall. We adjourned to a natural amphitheater below the camps to watch the evening's talent show, notable again for this opportunity it provided the master of ceremonies to show off his explicit language magnified by microphone. The audience, sitting on grassy banks around the stage, also enjoyed the chance to shout back insults, some well deserved.

The final event during my visit was a morning of horse races, held on a level stretch of ground beside the riverbed, where once again a grandstand and a high platform had been erected and the booming voice of the raucous track official was pumped through speakers so loudly that the ears of mules lay back in anguish. Amateur jockeys, professional horses, and numerous spectators milled up and down the track, while races were run in all directions. One white horse left his saddle and jockey at the starting gate and galloped away into the mountains, free at last to sort out his thoughts. In a mule race a stubborn entry ran his own race on his own track and won handily. A winner was disqualified, amid much thigh slapping, because he came from Texas, and in the "slow horse" race the loser carried off a gleaming trophy. Through it all I watched and warmed myself by the fire, wrapped in a small world, which for the moment, seemed large enough for me.

The Rancheros were preparing to ride out. Another camp awaited them a few mountains away, and the long line of riders was forming. I watched them the way a small boy watches his older brother leaving home for what must be a glorious excursion. And I made up my mind to become a Maverick. Those "seven wonderful days" must happen to me.

In June Jeremy and I drove to the nearby town of Santa Ynez for Tortilla Day, another of the Valley's annual social whirls. The main street of Santa Ynez is three blocks long, lined with ancient storefronts, a museum filled with Chumash baskets and pioneer furniture, and, on Tortilla Day, a huge tent where tacos and tortillas are served on paper plates. When we arrived, the street was lined with families waiting for the parade. On one side the town band, a dozen music lovers, sat on camp chairs blowing as loud as they could. Across from them a combination sound truck and speakers' stand was playing Herb Alpert records, also loud, while the master of ceremonies kept blowing into a microphone, saying, "Testing one two three four," apparently making the most of his one chance to hear himself all over town. Jeremy and I bought our tacos and beans and sat at a wooden table along the parade route to wait.

A Santa Ynez parade is, if nothing else, short. It can only go three blocks, so we saw most of it all at once. A high-school bugle corps, a group of children dressed to look like indians, a Chumash family smiling self-consciously, a stagecoach filled with the town's senior citizens, a disciplined posse of men from the Forest Service followed by Smokey the Bear, many riders on nervous horses, one *vaquero*, one goat, and an ear-shattering announcement from the master of ceremonies that one yellow purse, empty, had been found. That was Tortilla Day. We left before the prizes were announced. Somebody had locked the town rest rooms and we needed rest.

Horse shows seem to be about as frequent in our Valley as floor shows in places where there are fewer horses. Jeremy and I drove to the Alisal Guest Ranch one summer Saturday to see our first one. The spectacle was at first incongruous to me, somewhat like watching a couple in formal evening clothes coming home in bright sunshine. There are groups of boys and girls in proper equestrian attire, from velvet caps to polished English riding boots, mounted in a wide corral in a beautiful Western setting. While the judges look on from a high stand, the riders guided their polished mounts over a series of jumps, after which scores were announced through a loudspeaker. Flanking the corral was a corps of mothers and horse trailers, and tension and temper were mixed with smell of hay and saddle soap. The horses and the mothers were nervous, the children waited their turns. I noticed one mother scolding a white quarter horse which, at a moment like this, nonchalantly allowed his penis to dangle out for all to see. She was talking sternly to him.

We left after the winners were announced for that event, but I guess I knew how much Jeremy wanted to be part of it all. She would be.

We missed the annual Chumash barbecue on the Fourth of July, so I don't know whether they served missionaries or hot dogs, but there was always the Elks Rodeo, the Santa Claus Parade, and dozens of other events to look forward to. And I have yet to attend one of those dawn spectaculars where a group of friends serenades a sleeping couple at sunrise on their wedding anniversary. The couple, blasted awake by this good fellowship, is then expected to invite everybody in for breakfast. I'm keeping my anniversary quiet.

But there is something to be said for the social life of a country community. Perhaps it is refreshing because it is generated by people who still know how to amuse themselves. The ancient Chumash played their version of baseball on the Santa Barbara slopes hundreds of years ago. The early ranchers used horses and cattle for their games. And today we have no theater and only limited television. The search for pleasure goes on, and, like food, when we cannot buy it we grow our own.

It would take at least a year, I was told, to get to know people in the Valley. And I believed it, for after several months of ranching I could not really say I knew anybody except Jim Farmer. True, my Pancake House advisors seemed to enjoy their coffee a little more when I was there asking them about barbed wire, and I had a nodding acquaintance at the hardware store and the market, but I was not besieged with invitations to join my neighbors at their revels, if they had any. It should have been enough, I suppose, to relax at my own bonfire, play my own soulful harmonica, and gaze up at the stars, but now and then it wasn't. I was, especially about dusk on Saturday night, a lonesome cowboy.

I found my solution a couple of miles from the ranch in a town called Los Olivos, which consists of a flagpole set in the middle of two streets coming together through the tomato fields and flanked by a long bench where old men sit to watch the sun go down. Just beyond this hub of activity, like an oasis of light in a black desert, is Mattei's Tavern. And there it has been for nearly a hundred years. It seems that our railroad barons, busy linking the continent in the late nineteenth century, had a lapse of interest or funds while building the rail line between Los Angeles and San Francisco. The stretch between Santa Barbara and San Luis Obispo simply did not get built for many years, and passengers had the choice of strolling up and down the coast for ninety miles to board the train again or climbing on a Concord stage at Santa Barbara and bounding over the San Marcos Pass to meet a small railroad at Los Olivos. And so, Felix Mattei provided these rump-sprung travelers

46

an inn where they could dine and spend the night.

Old Mattei would be proud to know his tavern is still thriving, and if he were to visit it today he would feel right at home. His photograph is still on the wall, his guest books are still in the lobby, and his clock, stopped at one hour before midnight for some forgotten Cinderella, still waits for him to wind it. He might balk at the swinging gates of the bar, where there is a painting of a windblown nude, but otherwise Mattei's Tavern is still as it was. Its tree at Christmas is strung with popcorn and cranberries. Its huge fireplace burns the Valley's oak logs, and its men's room is out back, a refreshing stroll from the main building.

The first night I discovered the Tavern I also discovered that its new owner was a classmate of mine. How he had come from Princeton to oversee a stagecoach stop is his story, just as how I happened to be lost in Los Olivos is mine, but obviously he was a better innkeeper than I was a rancher at night. We sat and had a drink before I moved to an immaculately set table for a steak, and with few exceptions Jeremy and I have been going back every Saturday night since. The friends I was to take a year to assemble I have met at Mattei's. The welcome I receive, as do a hundred others like me, is now a part of my life in the Valley. Stepping through the door at sunset I feel I have earned its reward, which is warmth, good food, and the sounds of humanity. Leaving, I step once more into open country where skies were never so black nor stars so bright.

The first visitor to the ranch was my friend Lou, the accountant. I met him at the airport and drove him to the Valley to spend a Saturday with me, not without some uneasiness. But he was rubbing his hands in anticipation all the way. We arrived at noon, and while he removed his coat and tie in deference to the informality around him, I admitted I had only beer and cheese for lunch.

"Let's go to town," he said. "It's my treat."

We drove to Solvang and parked outside the Pancake House. Inside, he ordered a huge plate of Danish pancakes and sausage and said nothing until he had finished the last bite.

"Did you buy the sheep?" he asked suddenly.

"Cows, not sheep," I corrected him. "No, not yet."

"Any other income?"

"Only outgo so far," I admitted. "I've been fencing and putting in permanent pasture."

He puffed a little and headed for the cashier with the check. He walked next door then to one of the many Danish bakeries. Lou examined the counters filled with assorted pastries, cookies, bread, and cakes. He leaned toward the girl in Danish costume who had been watching him over a fruit cake. "How much is one of each?"

The girl was young and apparently unfamiliar with accountants. "One of each of which?"

"I'd like to try one of each of all these," Lou explained. "Then if I like something, maybe I'll come back and buy a dozen."

The girl and Lou worked their way down the counter, filling a pink box with one of each, skipping loaves of bread and bridal cakes. He paid her and we left. For the rest of the afternoon Lou carried his box with him, grunting occasionally, spilling crumbs wherever he went.

We went on a tour of my trees, Lou vainly searching for a walnut tree or any tree he could deduct. He tried a few berries and a dark, olive-sized fruit, spitting out each bite sadly, until he came to a fir tree tied up with ropes.

"It blew down in a storm," I told him.

"Why did you put it up again? You have plenty."

"I just felt like roping something, and a tree doesn't run away."

"We'll say it died," he announced.

I showed him my fence and let him stand on the road while I moved my pipes, but he seemed unimpressed with my ability and returned to the house for another pastry before I finished. We sat at the table late in the day, I gazing fondly at my field, Lou scanning the local paper, until it was time for dinner. Of course, he went with me to Mattei's and ate another huge meal. Later, we sat with Bud New, the owner, and I introduced Lou.

"What'll you take for it?" he asked Bud.

The innkeeper looked at him a little suspiciously. "I really couldn't name a price," he said. He should have been flattered. Lou ate the Danish pastry, but he didn't offer to buy the bakery.

We drove to the ranch and said good night. I wondered what Lou thought of my folly, prepared to defend the ranch if necessary. But at breakfast he told me.

"This is the best thing you every did," he said simply.

I decided that day to call my ranch Rancho Refugio. It had already become my refuge and much more than my responsibility. But how do you explain emotion? How do you describe the ingredients of such a fragile affair? I am glad Lou did not need an explanation.

I called Freddie from the ranch. "Lou says buying this place is the best thing I ever did," I told her.

"Did you explain why I wasn't there?" she asked.

"Of course," I said. "I told him cowboys make you sneeze and you're busy with Susie, and he sends his regards."

"Be sure to bring the lawnmower when you come home. And say hello to Lou."

She hung up sneezing.

4

"I would feel more optimistic about a bright future
for man if he spent less time proving he can
outwit nature and more time tasting her sweetness and
respecting her seniority."
- E. B. WHITE

Like many ranchers of the Old West, who shared their land with mountain lions, grizzlies, and wolves, I found a number of wild creatures there before me when I moved in. But unlike panthers and grizzlies, my wild co-owners suffered few casualties in the battle between us, if you can call our confrontation a battle. In fact, I'm sure they are all laughing their sort of laugh this minute, and certainly they are multiplying nicely, while I remain unmultiplied. I have always envied those naturalists and bird watchers who discover and describe more of the wonders of nature from their windows than most of us notice in a lifetime of travel. Their curiosity, patience, and seemingly boundless knowledge enables them to enjoy every atom around them. And they always know the names, English *and* Latin, for all they see. I am not one of them, yet I am surrounded by wildness, so I resolved to do my best.

Lacking binoculars, bird books, and feeders, I was off to a poor start with the birds who lived on my ranch. But my first weekend there I learned by my own methods to identify three crazy birds, and they are still the only three I am sure of. At first light one morning I was awakened by what sounded like a series of three blasts on a pop bottle, endlessly repeated from a Monterey pine outside my window. It was still too dark for anybody who enjoyed sleep to be up, but the three blasts seemed to be telling me something. Finally, I got it. As any fool should know, the three toots were Morse Code for the letter "O" and "O" stands for Owl. So it had to be an owl. He never did get around to sounding out the "W" and "L," perhaps because he didn't know the Code well enough, but then neither do I. I still hear him identifying himself most mornings, but I have never seen him. And I really don't mind his waking call. After all, any bird that assumes I know Morse Code can't be all bad.

Later that same morning I discovered that one of my neighbors keeps chickens. I had not yet met the Petersens, but their scouts were out, so it did not require any investigation on my part. The rooster walked over to my lawn and crowed for a solid hour, even after I got up and shouted "All right" at him. Thoreau goes on about "brave Chanticleer" and the great service he does mankind by getting everybody up early, but I never knew that roosters go from house to house, crowing endlessly and shattering sleep even for people they haven't met yet. He is an alarm clock which won't shut off, and by the time I chase him back home, a painful exercise in bare feet, I am up for the day.

There is another bird I have come to know. This one is small and slate gray, with beady eyes and a weight problem, and I am certain it must be a female. I first noticed her sitting on a branch just above my head making a "tsk tsk" sound of disapproval. I thought I might be working near her nest, so I moved, but she followed me all over the yard, hopping from one tree to the next, disapproving all the time and cocking an eye at me to be sure I heard her. I have heard female disapproval before and not from a fat gray superior bird, but I can't escape her. Whether I am working or relaxing, she is there making that damned "tsk" above me.

51

Those are the three birds I know: an owl that knows its name begins with "O," a rooster that doesn't know when to stop crowing, and a gray bird that doesn't like anything about me. On to other companions of mine.

If bird watchers are called "birders," are people who watch bugs called "buggers?" As a matter of fact, I am neither birder nor bugger.

My attitude toward insects has always been one of indifference, so long as they felt the same way. I have no hostility. I am content to allow the wasps' nests in the northwest eave of my ranch house to go undisturbed, and, on the other hand, to watch a potato bud devote four hours to an attempt to climb over a two-inch clump of dirt without helping him at all. I suppose I could give him a boost, but then what? He might get to depend on me.

In my first weeks as a rancher, however, I met a bug about which I could not be indifferent, partly because its chief aim in life seems to be to have a roof over its head - mine - and also because it doesn't come singly but by the thousands. I am referring to a small black insect called an earwig. It doesn't seem to want to bite, nor does it eat anything I like, but its urge to move in with me, touching as it might be to some, is anything but mutual. Earwigs in the first warm days of spring headed for every window and door in my house, as well as openings I never knew about before. Not content with having my roof over their little heads, they holed up in drawers and closets and under everything else, as if they felt that two roofs were better than one. After kicking a few out, I decided to attack with my vacuum cleaner. I might have known that this was the wrong method. In the first place, no earwig minds at all the exciting ride up the hose of a vacuum cleaner, and once inside, he feels he has accomplished his purpose, for he has his second roof made to order.

Stronger methods were indicated if I was to keep my earwigs outside, and I went to the hardware store for help. There I was handed a bottle of liquid labeled in large, black letters "Dieldrin." Anyone who has read *Silent Spring* knows all about dieldrin, and with Rachel Carson's dire warnings ringing in my ears I thanked the clerk and decided to stick to my own less lethal methods. Maybe spraying my doorstep with poisonous insecticide would not bring about, with the destruction of my earwigs, the death of the birds around me; certainly the chemical would hardly find its way into underground streams from my patio, but death, like life, is a chain reaction, and I would not be the one to light the fatal fuse. I swept the earwigs out the door, hoping they would head in another direction.

Many of my neighbors attack their weed patches with weed-killer, leaving stripes of burned orange vegetation around their yards, as if a rocket has been launched there. That this slash of ugliness is preferable to a spring growth of any living plant is strange to me, as are most of the human vetoes of nature's laws. If beauty does not lie in the eye of the beholder, then what is not beauty to his eye must not be beautiful at all, and there is a spray for it. Lupin, wild mustard, burr clover, even in my driveway, still look better to me alive.

The first animal visitor I recognized at the ranch was a large black-and-gray tomcat, stalking among the shrubs one evening. He paid me no attention, and I admire cats, so I left him alone. I have lived with a cat for sixteen years. Nicole calls her Nobugs, which is not accurate, and Susie, reckoning by human life span, figures she is one hundred and five years old. "But she doesn't look a day over eighty," Susie maintains. Cats are the only animals I know that can sit motionless in front of a bird they know they won't catch, then go home to dinner. Or wait patiently outside a door, knowing it will eventually open. My cat waits each morning for me to brush my teeth so that she can climb down into the sink and drink from the running faucet. She gets her ears wet and I have to wait, mouth filled with toothpaste, until she has quenched her thirst, but it is a ritual too ancient to disturb. So I welcomed my cat visitor and wished him luck. Had I known then what he was after and the absolute hopelessness of it all, I would have felt even more sympathy, but up to then I had not met a gopher.

I suppose it is difficult to imagine that any red-blooded American over forty has never seen a gopher, or even a gopher hole, but my acquaintance with things Western has come from movies and television, and not even Roy Rogers ever set out to rid the West of gophers. Come to think of it, if his writers had had to dream up one more episode he might have done it. Over the years he has captured everything except Dale.

Jim Farmer called me on Saturday. "You've got gophers in your lawn," he said. "I saw holes the other day when I was down there. Better buy some poison and get rid of them."

"I will," I said, and I did. That day I bought a can of gopher poison at the feed store (the one without the men's room) and hurried home to hunt for gopher holes. I found them, about a dozen small holes in the grass the size of golf balls, and carried the poison and a soupspoon to the lawn for my first bout with gophers. The poison turned out to be a gaudy mixture of raisins and brightly colored grain, red, green, and yellow. I assume gophers are color-blind, and anyway what can you see inside a gopher hole, but the spoon filled with poison looked quite festive. I put a heap inside each hole and covered it over with loose dirt and walked away. I'd never seen a gopher and I never hoped to see one.

I thought no more about it that day, but the next morning I went out to check the holes. I found to my dismay a sort of miniature golf course where no golf course should have been. Piles of loose dirt had risen in the night in various new locations, each surrounding a new hole. Apparently, my gophers had been up half the night establishing new quarters, the old holes abandoned, the poisonous treat left behind. It seemed like a sort of gopher Hallowe'en, and the trick was on me.

Mrs. di Vecchio dropped by the next weekend, searching for one of her children. "You've got gophers in your lawn," she commented as she walked around the yard calling.

"I know," I said. "What do you suggest?"

"Well," she told me, "they're tough to get rid of. I've found the best thing is to drown them. I stick a garden hose down the hole and just let it run."

I agreed to try it, and after she walked back up the road I approached a gopher hole with the hose at the ready. I stood there squirting water into the hole for ten minutes. Nothing happened, and the water disappeared into the caverns beneath the grass. Just as I was about to give up, I noticed a muddy movement at the entrance of the hole. "Aha," I cried, "it works. He's coming up for air." The lump gradually worked itself out of the hole until I saw him quite clearly. It was a great fat frog, blinking mud out of its eyes. Now either gophers, like princes, can turn into frogs when the going gets wet, or else frogs move into gopher holes like gypsies. At any rate, standing there watering a frog seemed to me a silly thing to be doing, and I abandoned the project. I would just get used to gophers in my lawn the way I had gotten used to my owl. Maybe in some wild burst of enthusiastic, misdirected tunneling they would finally dig their way right into the Petersens' yard. I went back and sat down in my favorite chair, and the frog made a single, grinding croak.

Beware of television ranching, you armchair cowboys who watch as I did the immaculate spreads in station-wagon commercials. A ranch house looking like a combination of a Western museum and a country club nestles in fields as smooth as putting greens, with fences of exotic woods, while beyond lie pastures filled with cattle, all of which, as Emerson wrote, "seem to have great and tranquil thoughts." The horses are always saddled and ready, and a plume of smoke curls up from the chimney as the boss casts a proprietary eye on all he surveys, confident that it will stay that way. If you rise from your chair and buy a ranch, you'll quickly learn that it won't stay that way. In fact, you may even have to learn how it got that way.

From the window of the house, my permanent pasture looked almost like the waving meadows on television. The grass, flecked with flowering wild mustard and lupin, was high and green, and six acres seemed to me at those moments like a world of my own. My excursions into the field to move irrigation pipes were exasperating, however. The rainbirds, my guides while the grass was young, disappeared, and a pipe hunt developed. Once found, the problem grew worse, for hauling pipes through tall grass is like pulling a garden hose through shrubbery. Often I simply sat down, disappearing myself, and puffed awhile, feeling foolish but mercifully hidden from sight.

But as the summer wore on and the rainless months continued, even my weekend watering was not enough. Burr clover died, then the taller of the flowering weeds turned brown, and soon my field took on a nibbled look and bare patches appeared. And it was in these patches that I first noticed gopher holes by the hundreds. Long after ploughing should have stopped, the gophers were out there digging furiously in the new grass. I dashed to the Pancake House for advice.

It was there that I first heard of a gopher machine. Nobody at the counter bothered to explain what it was or how it worked, but from the conversations I gathered that it was not a machine operated by gophers, nor had it been invented by one.

"Just what you need," Jim said. "Don't you think, Ed?"

"Yeah, that's what you need, all right," Ed agreed.

"It works just like a gopher," Jim explained. "Shore fools 'em, that gopher machine."

I began to have visions of a huge mechanical gopher, covered with fur, gnashing yellow steel teeth, making its way across my field eating gophers as it went along. But my friends considered the problem solved and went on to other topics, the usual ones being the price of beef, the price of hay, property taxes, and whether it would rain. I was left to discover the facts about gopher machines on my own. As I drove off, Jim Farmer called after me. "Let me know if you need any help with the gopher machine."

"I will Jim," I waved at him. "I hope it fools 'em."

"Oh, it will all right," he grinned. He does not grin often. I guess just the thought of fooling all those gophers was too much for him.

No, a gopher machine is not a giant gopher after all. I almost wish it were. At least it might have been easier to find one. I devoted a couple of Saturdays to my search, each time being referred by some farmer, scratching his head thoughtfully, to another who might have one, until I not only found one but discovered why they are so difficult to locate. They don't work.

A man named Sanchez at a neighboring ranch knew where I could rent a machine for a dollar an hour. He is the caretaker (I would prefer to call him foreman because it sounds ranchier) of a medium-sized place near mine. He has a marvelous clown face with a tuft of fur growing straight up from the top of his nose, like a goat's beard in reverse, and like the others, he scratched his head while he thought about it.

"Damn gophers," he said. "Yessir, I don't kill nothin' I can't eat, but them damn gophers, you can't eat 'em and you can't live with 'em. You tell Charlie I sent you."

I found Charlie and the machine rusting away in a shed near Los Olivos, and I managed to persuade him to bring it over to my field. As I stared at the gopher machine, I tried to figure out how it worked, but I have never understood any machinery more complicated than a shovel, so I'll describe it only as a wild assemblage of rods and chains, mounted on wheels to be drawn behind a tractor, with a torpedolike weapon in front for burrowing and another contraption behind for smoothing the ground above the tunnel. Poisoned green wheat resembling a breakfast cereal is deposited in the tunnel, and in theory the gopher, thinking he has found a new tunnel belonging to an affluent relative, plunges in and eats his way to Paradise. By surrounding a field with this phony gopher tunnel, sort of a Maginot Line is built which keeps out visiting gophers and confuses those already in residence.

"But all it takes," Charlie pointed out, "is one smart gopher and they're all back again."

"Then what good is the machine?" I asked.

"Well..." Charlie scratched. "Maybe that's why it's a little rusty."

Nevertheless, Charlie agreed to haul the gopher machine to my field one day the following week. I believe he did, but I have no way of knowing, except that he sent me a bill. I saw no trace of the poisonous tunnel, of course, and I never yet had seen a gopher, so all I had to go by were the new mounds of dirt and the thousands of old holes. But I knew my gophers were still with me and that

Charlie had been right. All it takes is one smart gopher.

But, in a way I am glad. If man could build a better gopher hole than a gopher can, there would be no stopping us. Sawhorses would be winning races, scarecrows would become diplomats, dolls would be delinquents. And, too, the world is better off with rusty gopher machines and smart gophers. When we realize at last that we cannot build an animal, perhaps we will be less determined to destroy the ones we have.

My objective that first year was to raise grass, not gophers, so that in time I could go on to cattle and horses, and it seemed to me as I walked through my pasture that it was becoming less and less permanent. Now I came across great craters surrounded by mounds of dirt high enough to be seen from the house. These, certainly, were not gopher holes unless my gophers had united. Something was turning my pasture into terrain resembling the surface of the moon. What would Lorne Greene do?

I went back for more advice to the Pancake House where my friend Jim Farmer and his Western coffee klatsch were in session. They all owned large ranches, which apparently ran themselves while these men sat sipping coffee, their Western hats hanging in a line on the wall behind them, their boots, worn and comfortable, tucked under the stools. I was welcome always, but I was not, like them, a rancher whose problems took care of themselves. I had no hat to hang on the wall with theirs, no herds to sell, no horse to ride.

"How'd the gopher machine work?" Jim asked, while the others flexed lean jaws like men who were about to ride shotgun on the morning stage.

"I've still got gophers," I said. "And they seem to be growing. Now they're digging caves instead of holes."

"Oh, you must have badgers too," Ed McCarty volunteered.

"Badgers!"

"Yea. They go after gophers. You want to get rid of them before you put in livestock. They're mean, badgers."

I sipped my coffee and waited for a solution I knew would come.

"Hard to get 'em though," Jim added.

"Got a dog?" Ed wondered.

I nodded, wondering if he thought my fat collie could be persuaded to squeeze himself into a badger hole.

"Then I wouldn't use eggs, would you, Jim?"

"Naw, dog'll get eggs. Wouldn't want your dog to eat an egg filled with strychnine. Fella I know used to use the Sunday paper. He'd stuff the paper down the hole. Badger couldn't work his way through that."

"I can't either," I agreed. "I only do the puzzle."

Nobody laughed. My rancher friends aren't much for laughing. I guess, like Ward Bond and James Arness, they all have comical sidekicks who provide the humor while they stare off to the horizon, watching for Indians.

"Tell you what you do," Jim said slowly. "Go down to the agriculture office in the sheriff's station and tell 'em you got badgers. They'll send a man out. They don't even charge you."

I settled for that solution and left them to their coffee. Why didn't they have badgers and gophers and earwigs? Why did I have to struggle with one plague after another? Perhaps these invaders, like lions, single out the weakest in the herd and go after him. I felt like a slow gazelle.

I stopped off at the County Agricultural Department's Solvang office where I found a girl sitting behind piles of pamphlets. She did not look like anyone who could dispose of a badger, but you never know in this country. Even the librarian looks leathery. I explained my problem, and, just as Farmer predicted, she promised to send someone over.

"What'll he do?" I asked her, visions of a badger machine unavoidable.

She looked up over a stack of pamphlets on cattle diseases and smiled. "He'll show you," she said.

I thanked her and drove back to the ranch.

A county truck pulled into my driveway just before lunch, and a young man with an imposing emblem on his shirt sleeve and an air of competence common among people who wear emblems jumped down and grinned.

"Badger problem?" he asked.

"They're plowing up my field," I told him. In spite of his self-assurance and his emblem I wondered what he could do. My collie sniffed him carefully as he began opening boxes on the side of his truck.

"I've had pretty good luck lately with bombs," he told me.

He went on with his preparations, opening small boxes, biting off the ends of capsules, attaching small fuses. I watched and wondered, as always, for I am naturally suspicious of chemical warfare. Our progress in this area seems a bit haphazard to me, for we now sterilize rats on purpose and pelicans by mistake. Only the week before a light plane, loaded with spray, had buzzed me all day on its way to a walnut grove beyond my pasture. It made trip after trip between the walnuts and its source of supply. But as it came in for another pass at the walnuts, spray guns at the ready, it was no more than a few feet above my head, which for all I know may have looked from the air like a walnut. Now bombs!

When he was ready, we walked out into the field, leaving my dog shut inside the house. There before us were the mounds of loose dirt every few feet. The badger bomber moved from one to the other until he found one obviously excavated during the previous night. Then he knelt down and placed his small bomb far inside the hole. When all was ready, he lit the fuse, kicked as much dirt back down the hole as he could, and backed away. A muffled explosion, felt rather than heard, followed, and a plume of blue smoke crawled out through the dirt. At last I had to ask the inevitable question.

"How do you know the badger is in there?"

The bomber grinned again. "I know he was there last night," he said. "He spends the day in one of these new holes, and the gas in the bombs will get him. We'll try one more just in case."

He walked off across the field looking for another fresh mound of dirt, while I followed at a distance, looking back dubiously at the site of the last explosion. We found another easily. My badger or badgers spent active nights out there in the moonlight and must have been exhausted by morning. But not the badger

60

bomber. He was briskly setting another bomb down a hole, lighting matches and kicking dirt like a man who slept soundly in a highrise apartment. Another went off, and more of the blue smoke curled out of the ground.

"That ought to do it," he announced and headed back across the field to his truck, anxious to be on his way to a different challenge. I signed a paper without reading it, which probably absolved him of all blame, thanked him, and retreated to my house. It had all been done so quickly, so efficiently. My enemy, which I had never seen, had been met and conquered while he slept by tossing gas bombs into his bedroom, but I did not feel heroic. I had come to this peaceful spot to join him and had ended up fighting him instead. And it could all have been solved so easily without a sneak attack on a sleeping victim. If my badger would cover up his holes again, there would be no danger to livestock, no lumps and cavities across my pasture. But badgers are like the rest of us. The fun is in making the mess, not in cleaning it up. Badgers are not golfers. They won't replace the divots.

My Sunday mornings as a rancher begin early, helped along first by my owl and then by the rooster, but they progress slowly as do I. The Saturday pressure of having everything to do at once is off, and I have no need to dash from one job to the next, kicking earwigs, turning on sprinklers, going to the dump. They are mornings when I am as close to control as I ever am, and while something always needs to be done, it does not have to be done before breakfast and on the run. The morning after the badger bomber had done his work I walked out into the pasture, as always gazing proudly at the whole expanse, imagining peaceful herds to come and the whinny of recognition from my faithful horse. But it is difficult to cast a satisfied gaze across your own Western acres with one foot sunk to the shin in a badger hole. A huge hole, hidden in the grass, had trapped me, and as I wrenched my foot out of the hole I noticed other new mounds around me. Furious excavating had gone on all night, old mounds and new were everywhere, and my "spread" was so pocked that my imaginary cattle would have had to be gymnasts to walk through the field.

I ran for the stable, my Sunday calm shattered. I found a shovel and dashed back to the field where I began to fill in badger holes as if my life depended on it. Dirt flew, mounds were stuffed back into holes again, and I was gasping. I filled in twelve badger caves without letup and then rested, trying to compute the chances I had of success. If a badger digs six holes a night and I cover a dozen holes a day, I figured it would take me about three years to catch up. That was not quite what I had in mind when I bought the ranch. I was certain that Jimmy Stewart, who owns a large ranch at the other end of my road, wasn't out there with a shovel, but perhaps if I did it early in the morning nobody would see me. I could still swagger into the Pancake House to discuss cattle prices with those self-satisfied ranchers after I had filled my daily quota of holes.

Jeremy called from the fence. "What are you doing, Daddy?"

"I'm filling in badger holes," I cried. "What else is there to do on Sunday morning?"

"Won't they just dig more?" she asked, hoping, I'm sure, that I wouldn't throw any dirt in their little eyes.

I attacked the nearest heap with a vengeance. "Not as fast as I can cover them up," I told her. I filled in my dozen and felt satisfied. Perhaps I was becoming a rancher after all. All I had to do was close up abandoned badger holes for the rest of the summer. After all, ranching is not all roping and tying, ti-yi.

Charles Lindbergh wrote not long ago that "the human future depends on our ability to combine the knowledge of science with the wisdom of wildness." Here in my corner of the West I am not worried about the wisdom of wildness. There seems to be no danger, at least from me, and nature's balance is being nicely maintained.

But I missed the thunder of tiny hooves. It was time for a greater challenge, time to start building my herd.

5

"I am wont to think that men are
not so much the keepers of herds
as herds are the keepers of men."
- THOREAU

Winter at the ranch was a period of restless waiting. After a spring and summer of preparation, seeding and irrigating my pasture and watching it bloom under my hand, fencing the land and nursing lawn and trees through hot sunny weeks, suddenly the Valley winter arrived in December, and everything else stopped, so I had to stop also. Under gray morning skies and cool sun in the afternoons my pasture, even with a few early rains, slept, and each night frost nipped the lawn until it to gave up and turned a darker, lifeless green. Gone were gophers and badgers to their lower berths, and the birches I was so proud of were cold white sticks. I felt, during these weeks, as an insomniac must feel at three o'clock in the morning, awake while everybody else is asleep, and there was nothing to do but wait.

But spring in Santa Ynez ignores the calendar, and by February the first jonquil shoots circled the bare birches. I noticed one

Saturday a green patina in the corral and on the dirt path leading to the stables, and by the following week, after another rain things began to happen. Now there was a light blanket of early grass in the bare places, and my pasture, soaked at no charge, came to life.

Jeremy and I were still building fires to warm the house at night and leaving green footprints on the frosty lawn in the morning, but winter was over, and the second spring was here.

"Would cows mind the cold nights?" Jeremy asked. "It's really warm in the afternoon."

"I don't think they would," I told her.

"Then why don't we..."

"We will," I said. The preparation was over. It was time for the Townsend herd to arrive. "Move 'em on in!" I shouted, just as Eric Fleming used to do.

"Daddy!" Jeremy laughed.

The laws of California require that all cattle owners register their brands with the Department of Agriculture. I don't know whether this is to frighten away rustlers or to support the Department of Agriculture, but it was heady information to me, and I immediately drove to the Santa Ynez Stockyards to pick up an application for my brand.

I discovered that I was supposed to submit a design of my own to Sacramento, and if my choice was not already registered, it would become forever mine. "That's the Townsend brand," I could hear old hands saying whenever they saw it. "He owns a spread south o' here." The entire family rose to the challenge, and we sat down at my table at the ranch to design a brand - and somehow to include everybody's initials in it. Our first attempts looked more like the coat of arms of a small Arabian country than anything that might end up on a cow's hip, but eventually we settled on something that looked like this:

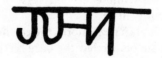

I quickly mailed in the design with my check and waited impatiently for word from the Department. In a couple of weeks back came my Certificate of Cattle Branch Registration No. 105292 and the approval branch, which had been altered by somebody to look like this:

Well, it wasn't exactly my idea of a brand that would go down in history. In fact, the more I looked at it the more I thought it looked like a mushroom on a toothpick. But my cattle would wear it with pride on their right hips. I began to make plans to have it painted on the side of my car and maybe burned into the panelling on the walls of the ranch. The Townsend brand was a matter of California history.

Kris Klibo, a giant Dane, is the blacksmith in the Valley, and I went to him for my branding iron. I drove to his shop in the town of Buellton one Saturday morning, the Sacramento version of my design clutched in my hand. His shop turned out to be a long shed of corrugated iron filled, it seemed to me, with all of the scrap that had accumulated since the Industrial Revolution. There was a thick film of black dust on everything, and the light from a single sooty bulb illuminated an old desk piled with papers at the far end. A sudden shower of sparks off in the gloom pinpointed Kris, who was welding a couple of pieces of old iron into something that looked exactly like a piece of old iron. He lifted his goggles to the greasy cap that covered part of his reddish hair, and I waited and watched while he pounded the iron, shaping it carefully and finally plunging it into a pail of dirty water. He left his creation and went off in search of something, never glancing my way at all.

After a while he reappeared and came toward me.

"I need a branding iron," I said quickly, while I had him more or less in sight. I held out the green paper with the design drawn on it in black ink, and he reached out a giant hand with, I noticed, a heavily bandaged thumb. He looked at the design for a long time, and finally said, "That's quite a brand you got there. You plan to brand your cattle or broil 'em?"

"It is a little complicated," I admitted. "Sacramento, you know."

He looked at me, then at the design, then back to me as if he never heard of the place. "Broke my thumb last week," he said, shoving the blackened bandage at me. "Know what I asked the doc when he set it?"

"No, I don't," I answered, stepping back to keep the thumb from brushing my nose.

He looked at me without expression. "I asked him if I'd be able to play the mandolin when the bone knit. He said, 'Why, of course you can, Kris.' I said, 'That's good, Doc, because I've always wanted to play the mandolin.'"

I laughed, but Kris didn't. He just watched me laugh.

"How long do you think it will take to make it?" I asked, trying to get back to my brand.

"'Bout an hour."

"Can I pick it up next Saturday?"

"Nope. Goin' fishin' next week. Make it two weeks."

I agreed to come back in two weeks and thanked him. As I walked out into the bright sunlight again, he called after me. "I do play the trombone."

I guess he does. He probably made it in that iron mine of his out of old jokes soldered together.

From the freeway above Buellton the stockyards look like an abandoned farm, surrounded by cattle pens of weathered boards. In fact, six days each week the whole place seems about to succumb to the dozen rainy days and the eroding sunshine to sink back into the barren landscape. But on Thursdays the cattle pens are filled, each cubicle crammed with livestock, each animal wearing on its rear a yellow paper tag with a black number printed on it. The aging building through which the stock is driven is also busy on Thursdays. Pickups and cattle vans are parked all around it, and men stand in small groups, buyers and sellers, waiting for the signal to enter, to sit in the grandstand facing the runway and the auctioneer, watching as animals enter through the gate on the right side of the building, pause to be looked over, and exit at the left onto a platform where they are weighed.

On a Thursday soon after our decision, I arranged to meet Nielson Downs at the yards. Downs, a cattle buyer for many ranches in the area, had agreed to buy and deliver my first herd of cattle for me, and I soon had reason to admit I was not ready for this experience. I drove up shortly before noon and parked among the pickups. Then, on being told that Nielson was over looking at the cattle, I went to the pens.

Downs, a rangy, good-natured man, saw me coming and waved. "We're gonna climb up and have a look," he called, and up he went to walk along the narrow boards at the top of the maze of cattle pens. I climbed up too, not wanting to admit that I had never strolled along the top of a fence before, looking down on the backs of cows and wondering when I would fall into a group of them and probably be sold before I could climb out again.

Nielson waved at me, and I weaved along to a pen where several black Angus calves were bellowing, their paper identifications looked like price tags to be torn off later by their buyers.

"They look pretty good to me," he said. "Just what you want."

One of the calves made a terrible racket. The others looked up at us with certain misgivings, and I looked down and them and felt dizzy. "How much do they weigh?"

"Oh, about four hundred," he said. "You don't want 'em any smaller than that."

"I don't?"

"Naw. They're good ones. We'll try to get 'em." He took out a pen and wrote the numbers down on the palm of his hand. I wondered if he just didn't have any paper, but when you don't know anything about the cattle business and want to hide it from as many people as possible, you learn to ask few questions and to do a lot of nodding and grunting. We climbed back down and went to the hot dog stand for lunch.

Promptly at twelve thirty the auction began, and we all drifted into the shed to sit in the grandstand. It was a wild scene. The big gate would open at the right, a thundering herd would enter. The auctioneer, standing at a crude rostrum, nodding and waving to friends in the audience, suddenly let out a stream of gibberish into a microphone. Drivers down among the cattle cracked small whips, cows mooed their confusion, wooden walls creaked as they slammed against them, and, suddenly, the gate at the left opened, and the cattle ran through. The first sale was over.

Next to me Nielson just sat.

"Fella behind us bought the lot for twenty-six cents a pound," Downs explained. You could have fooled me. I didn't see any one of the thirty men around us move a muscle. I didn't hear a price mentioned, and the whole transaction happened in no more than a minute. But, gradually, I learned as we watched animals singly and in groups charge into the building that the auctioneer, like that babbler in the old Lucky Strike commercials, was shouting prices, beginning low and working up, watching for a sign from the buyers at each new price, and finally shouting "Sold" when he couldn't find a higher bid. He still sounded like an outboard motor to me, and the cattle didn't seem to understand much either, but everybody else did.

After a couple of hours, a group of Angus calves stumbled out of the sunlight into the dark room, and I noticed Nielson coming to life. The calves were driven past the auctioneer whips cracking, men shouting silly things like "Hi" and "Ho" at them, and Downs looking first at his palm, then at the calves. They were out the door before I got a chance to decipher the price.

"You just bought three calves," Nielson announced, getting to his feet. "Pretty good price too. Come on."

He led the way down to the door and around the building just in time for me to see a couple of grizzled cowboys on sleepy ponies herding the calves into a pen on the left side of the building. The bony bottoms of my herd bounced along the path toward the pen, and I felt like a landlubber who has just seen himself buy a yacht. Downs told me he would stick around to brand the cows. (He had my branding iron, and I would not have stayed for that job for all the cows in the world.)

"I'll get 'em over to your place tomorrow," he promised. "They'll be in the field when you come up Saturday."

I thanked him, made out a check for $325.00 to the Santa Ynez Stockyard, and drove slowly down the road. I had done it, by God. I could hardly wait for Saturday.

The next day I went shopping for my first pair of Western boots. Los Angeles has many stores specializing in Western clothes, string ties, pearl-button shirts, and wide belts, Western hats and boots, and even, for the Beverly Hills cowboys, formal evening wear complete with patent leather boots and diamond horseshoe cufflinks. I did not want to dress like Hoot Gibson, but I confess to a secret desire to wear as many of these duds as a middle-aged ersatz cowboy might get away with, and I felt that I had at least earned my boots, so to speak. The clerk at the store I chose, wearing a shirt with his name in sequins across it, asked if I had ever worn boots before, and, honest to the end, I admitted I had not. He brought me a pair he said were the kind "to begin with" and showed me how to put them on. They wouldn't go on.

He came back and sprinkled talcum powder into the boots, and I tried again. After squeezing and swaying for some time, the boots were on and felt, I agreed, very comfortable. In fact, they felt so good I decided to wear them home. "Remember that little trick," the clerk called after me. "Just use a little powder."

My children laughed more than necessary when I walked in in my new boots, but I poured a drink, wobbled to a chair and ignored them. All went well until it was time to take them off. Then I simply couldn't. The powder was no help, except that I began to smell better. Wedging my foot in various tight places and pulling didn't help either. It was impossible. I began to see why my old Western heroes had died with their boots on. They couldn't take them off.

I called for help and got Jeremy and Nicole to pull, while I

69

braced myself on the bed. Finally, off they came, but my daughters were flushed and panting, and I felt foolish. I decided to take plenty of talcum powder along the next day, even if it was lavender and expensive. I was up and on the road at dawn on Saturday for the two-hour trip to the ranch. Jeremy and a friend of hers went with me, and the sun had never seemed brighter, the day more promising. We drove into the dirt road to the ranch before nine and looked for three black shapes in the tall grass.

"Where are they?" Jeremy asked.

"Probably at the water trough behind the house," I answered, but I was not certain myself. We parked and ran out to the corral. No calves. They weren't there. I hurried back to the house to call Nielson Downs and located him at one of several places he works. When I told him the calves were gone, he said, too calmly for me, "Well, they musta got out. I'll be over as soon as I can. You look around for em."

Look around! He made it sound as though I had misplaced a cufflink. Where do you look around for three four-hundred-pound calves? But Jeremy burst in just then with news that the calves were at the far end of the adjacent field, grazing contentedly. We all dashed out into my field and found, in the far corner, a hole in the barbed wire fence about the size of a basketball. Apparently my steers had gone through this hole.

We ran across some thirty acres of grass belonging to a neighbor to the steers, who glanced suspiciously at us and then went back to breakfast. "Move around them," I directed my two young helpers, "and then walk slowly toward them."

We surrounded the three-steer herd on three sides and started them off across the field toward the hole in the fence. I suddenly remembered that this was my first roundup and shouted "Ho" once or twice, not loud enough to attract their attention, but loud enough to feel good myself. They trotted along fine until we came to the fence. Then they simply stopped and snorted. I realize that, like putting a cork back into a champagne bottle, it was one thing to go out through that little hole when they wanted to, but something else to go back through it when they didn't want to. They seemed to know this too, and promptly turned and charged back at us. I shouted "Ho" again, louder this time, but they went right past me until, at a safe distance, they settled to grazing.

At this point I saw Nielson coming across the field on foot, followed by another man on horseback. "We'll drive 'em out of the other field and bring 'em down the road," he called. "You just wait and open the gate when I tell you." We waited.

The old cowboy rode off down the road and through the gate into the field where the calves were. The minute he reached them they began to run along in front of him like well-behaved children. He took them through the gate and up along the road in single file until they reached my driveway, where Nielson turned them. He waved for me to open the gate and stand back, and down the path they came and back through the gate and into the field. I closed the gate and hurried over to help him patch the hole with bailing wire, and again the calves ate as if this had not been one of the great round-ups in memory.

When we were back at the gate I offered to pay the cowboy, whose name I never did hear, but he waved it away. He sat on his horse rolling a cigarette with one hand, holding the reins in the other, and grinned. "No charge for that," he said as if my first round-up wasn't really worth the name. Then he rode off down the road.

The calves stayed home the rest of the day, and we watched them until it was too dark to see them any longer silhouetted against the darkening field. Then we went in to eat our dinner. We ate hamburgers which Jeremy had cooked, but I noticed that night for the first time that she was looking at her food a little suspiciously.

"Do hamburgers come from steers?" she asked quietly.

"No, they come from supermarkets," I told her, but I knew, I knew.

"Help me take my boots off," I said to the girls, hoping to change the subject.

My two young cowhands grabbed a boot apiece and pulled until they were purple and gasping and the boots were off.

71

Jeremy, sitting on the bedroom floor, boot in hand, suddenly looked worried again. "What will happen to them during the week?" she asked. "We're never here then to feed them."

I was ready for that, schooled as I had been for months at the counter in the Pancake House. "That's what the permanent pasture is for," I explained, "and the water trough. All steers need is grass and water. If I move the pipes around fast enough to keep the grass growing and the water trough doesn't leak, they'll be happy."

Jeremy, used to the dependence of cats and dogs on her handouts, would worry for a while about three steers that really didn't need her from Sunday to Friday. I would worry too. But Jim Farmer was never wrong. "Don't worry," he had said.

"Don't worry," I repeated to Jeremy.

There are, I have read, numerous diseases common among cows and many of these spell doom for them. There is, however, only one disease fatal to the cattle owner, which he alone can catch. I didn't know it, but the first subtle signs of this disease, known variously as "falling in love with a cow" or "getting sentimental over steers" appeared only a week after my three calves moved in. My daughter announced the following weekend, when we were reading about Angus cattle, that she had named the steers.

"I told you not to get to like them," I reminded her. "They're a business, a tax deduction."

Jeremy looked at me in a way she has, a look that says quite simply, "You know you don't believe that any more than I do."

"What are their names?" I asked, wishing I didn't have to know.

"Well, the littlest one is Corporal Salt. He's really cute. Then the next littlest one is Sergeant Pepper, and the biggest one is Lieutenant Barley. The only trouble is I can't always tell the difference between Sergeant Pepper and Lieutenant Barley."

Later that day I saw Jeremy out in the field holding a few blades of grass toward the smallest one, which remained at a safe distance from her but was obviously curious. They all watched as she moved a step nearer, and then back off a step themselves, but only a step.

72

"That kid is going to make pets out of them," I muttered and thought about Lou and his sharpened pencils. But they did look gentle and pleased.

I think it was only a weekend or two later that Jeremy announced proudly that Corporal Salt knew his name. That's ridiculous, I said to myself. They're dumb, dumb, dumb. They're big, black lawnmowers that gain a pound of steak a day. They're bundles of roast beef with runny noses.

Jeremy insisted. "He really does, Daddy. He looks up when I call him. The others don't know their names yet, though."

"That's encouraging," I said. "How about putting the steaks on for dinner?"

"Oh, Daddy," Jeremy laughed. "That's different."

We ate together in silence, looking out across the field at Corporal, Sergeant, and Lieutenant. That is the moment when the sun sits just above the foothills and the lawn is shadowed to a dark velvet texture by the trees around the house, while just beyond the fence our field is yellow-green with sunlight. The "geography of hope" for mankind may be, as Joseph Wood Krutch has suggested, that part of the earth where he has yet to plant his weeds of civilization, but for me the geography of hope is that small piece of California outside my window where I am allowed to watch in silence as day and night blend upon the grass. The black, stubby shapes of steers in the center of the field seemed to give the ranch a new personality for me, the same way a room changes when it is furnished or a face when it smiles. The steers were mine, content to feed off my land, and yet they were free to enjoy it all, safe from the cracking terror of the stockyards for a year. I sat back and watched and felt good.

Later, after Jeremy had pulled off my boots and we were ready for bed, she stopped at my bedroom door. "Daddy, you know what?"

I looked up. "What?"

"Corporal has the longest eyelashes I ever saw."

"Good night, Stub," I said and put out the light.

In May it was time to irrigate the pasture again, but this time I had three four-legged assistants, and moving the pipes became a game between me and the steers. They began by watching, I suppose to get the hang of it for themselves. As soon as they realized that the long, aluminum pipes moving through the grass were not threatening them they went out of their way to stand over them so that I had to pull the pipes out form under the steers, who simply chewed and blinked their long eyelashes. When the pipes were set up in the new row, ready to spray the field, but before I could get to the end of the field where the water outlet was, my three assistants moved over the pipes and began to scratch their chins on the rainbirds. This, of course, caused the rainbirds to fall over and the pipes to separate from each other, so I had to return and set up the row again. The conclusion of our game arrived when, pipes linked and rainbirds erect once more, I would shout "Back" to the steers, startling them briefly, then run to the end of the field to turn on the water. Sometimes it worked. Sometimes it took several tries, but when you keep pets you have to expect some inconvenience.

By the end of October the field was eaten to stubble. The steers were fat and unworried, and the rains would come soon. But frost would also come again, and it was time to buy hay for my herd. This, although I did not know it then, was to be the final link in our love affair, which was to turn them into close friends rather than deductions.

I started off feeding them a couple of pitchforks of hay for dinner on Fridays, breakfast early on Saturday, and dinner again Saturday nights. At first, they marched to the water trough as they always do just before sunset and discovered, like children on Christmas morning, a surprise pile of hay beside it. But it only took a weekend before they got the idea that my presence meant hay.

By this time the shortened days of November and December found me feeding them their Friday dinners in darkness, carrying loads of hay from the stable to the trough with a flashlight hung from my belt to light the way. And by this time my three steers were watching and waiting. As I turned into the long driveway, they would let out bellows of greeting and come trotting across the field to stand waiting, their black noses poking through the fence rails. At first light in the morning they marched down again, this time to stand mooing along the fence outside my bedroom window. It got so that I could not bear to eat my own breakfast before they had theirs, so I would rush out to the stable for hay and they would move along to the trough to wait and roar like three black ocean liners.

The bond that feeding time established between me and the steers over the winter months seemed unbreakable. As new grass grew in the field after heavy rains and food was plentiful, I considered cutting off their hay supply, but they would have none of it. Now they recognized my car and lifted their voices in salutation each time I drove down the road. They also lifted their noses to be scratched each time I leaned across the fence, and when I entered the field to repair some fences one Saturday, they followed like puppies, nuzzling and bumping me, never more than a step behind me wherever I went. Even I could tell them apart by now, and to them I was the great provider. I became so sentimental one Saturday after Corporal licked me that I ran out and bought them a new salt block. At least I didn't ask the feed store clerk to wrap it as a gift.

Nielson Downs called me in May. The steers had been in my field more than a year and were fat now with burr clover, weighing between seven and eight hundred pounds. I was still feeding them hay because I could not bear to see their faces staring at me through the fence or to hear their plaintive cries, but they didn't need hay any more than I did. Their woolly winter coats were being rubbed off and their flies were back. Spring had come again and, frankly, I dreaded it.

"Seems to me you'd be wanting to sell those steers and maybe get some new ones," Downs said.

"I guess it's time, isn't it?" I answered.

"Oh, sure," he said. "They'd be prime beef now and prices are high. You'll have to pay a lot more for calves, but maybe you should get half a dozen this time."

"That was my plan," I told him. "But wouldn't it be a good idea to get three calves now and settle them before we sell these?"

Downs liked my idea. Little did he know my reasons for suggesting it, and I had no plan to tell him. "Then let's do it," I said, feeling that I had gotten away with it. "See what you can pick up for me at the yards."

Originally it had been my intention to sell my first herd and use the money, approximately twice what I had paid for them a year earlier, to buy twice as many now. Lou would approve of that sort of plan, for it not only provided me with the necessary profit, but it showed my intention to plunge further into the cattle business each year. But, of course, that was before Corporal's long eyelashes and Sergeant's wet nose and Lieutenant's affectionate shoving had changed me from a cattle owner into a sentimental stepfather. Now the call from Downs jolted me back to reality and another retreat from it. Three young calves in the field might soften the blow, I thought, and I would have them to turn to when the others were gone. And perhaps six steers would seem more like a herd than a family.

To make matters worse, I had been reading Mel Morse's *Ordeal of the Animals*, a book so shattering to a lover of animals that I could only get through a few pages at a time. In his chapter on slaughterhouses, he went into vivid detail about such things as the poleax, the shackle, and the hoist, and I thought about my cattle sale with increasing uneasiness. Morse did say that a more or less painless slaughter of cattle was possible, using such devices as carbon dioxide gas or electric stunning, but he dashed my hopes by reminding me that these methods were more expensive and that slaughterhouses, inured to it all and rarely inspected, simply did not bother.

"How old do cows get?" Jeremy asked me after Downs's call.

"I doubt if anyone knows," I told her. "They usually don't die of old age."

"Ours will," she said.

"Come on, Stub," I cried. "You know we have to sell them."

It could have been painless for me, at least. All I had to do was tell Downs to pick them up some Thursday while I was off in Los Angeles eating a steak sandwich. When I returned to the ranch,

76

they would be gone, and I would never know. But that was just it! I wouldn't know and the guilt gnawed me.

I decided to call the Department of Agriculture office in Los Angeles and reached a Mr. Jennings. I explained my dilemma to him, and, at first he was quite encouraging. He referred to such things as the Packers and Stockyards Act and the Humane Slaughter laws. No steer, he assured me, could be sold to the Federal government unless these laws had been observed, and, moreover, California had its own laws governing the slaughter of animals. "But you know how people get when they work in those placed," he said gloomily. Careless, I thought, and who is to know? And I remembered Mel Morse's words on the subject. And I thought of Corporal running up to me for hay. And I crumpled into my hard chair. What happened to that rangy cattleman I thought I was? Steely muscles, cold blue eyes, filled with the spirit that conquered the West. Why hadn't I tried walnuts? Even I can slaughter a walnut without a second thought.

Jeremy and I returned to the ranch that Friday, late in the afternoon when the sun was again illuminating the field. There were Corporal, Sergeant, and Lieutenant, their heads lifted at the sight of my car on the road. And behind them in the tall grass were three smaller black shapes.

"They're here," Jeremy shouted.

As we drove to the house, the three older steers trotted along behind us, mooing with pleasure. The three small ones waited and wondered for a moment. Then they came along too, and by the time I appeared at the trough with my fork filled with hay six noses were on the rail.

Having fed my herd I returned to my favorite spot: my chair overlooking the best of both worlds, tame and wild, that lay beyond the window. On the shadowed lawn my collie, Fernando, lay cooling himself, and all was order and beauty as a man creates his own beauty out of the raw materials he is given. Just beyond lay another kind of beauty - a field of uneven growth, chewed by cattle, ploughed by gophers, patrolled by birds of a dozen species. And beyond the field the foothills still held sunlight and animals of a wilder order. It all stretched before me in slices of green and yellow and brown, leading away from me and my chair to the beginnings of life itself on the rocks of a distant peak. That I could look across this wedge of geography, that I could even cross from one wildness to the next as a visitor, just as a coyote on the far peak could cross toward me, seemed enough to ask. A weasel suddenly appeared in the field, as motionless as a small orange-and-white snake, then collapsed into the grass in his search for dinner. The cattle started back along the fence to find a spot to rest. Fernando watched them from the lawn without raising his head. Nobody wanted to intrude.

"Ready for dinner?" Jeremy asked.

"Whenever you are," I told her.

She went into the kitchen, and I put an Ives symphony on the phonograph. But softly. I wanted to be able to hear Jeremy when she announced the names of the three new calves.

6

"Joy, thou shining spark of God..."
- FRIEDRICH VON SCHILLER

Jeremy sat with me at our round table. Two months after our first herd had moved in they were "settled," as we cattlemen say. In other words, they grazed together while the dew lay on the pasture sweetening the grass, they lay in the pools of shade along the edges of the fence in the heat of the day, and at sunset they walked single file down to the water trough for what I suppose must be a calf cocktail hour. They had accepted things and relaxed. And so we relaxed, I with a book and my own cocktail, and Jeremy reading next to me. But Jeremy was then not much of a reader, and I wondered about the thick volume she held propped against the edge of the table. Her long blonde hair fell forward so that all I could see was the rounded end of her nose, and I found myself watching her instead of my own book. She was twelve, tall, blue-eyed, pretty, and right at the edge of adolescence. I could see in her both the little girl I knew and the first signs of the adult I hoped to know. I thought of her for the first time that evening in terms of her group and tried to relate what I knew of her to what I had read about her generation.

She had the energy of youth, that little extra push Emerson described as necessary to all young animals, and the confidence in a limitless future. She had not yet been recruited for protests and mobilizations, where so many of her contemporaries seem to be giving up so much precious freedom to be themselves, their backs to the future in order to fight what they don't like about our past. I suppose there is strength in numbers. The bees and the ants do pretty well, but one bee or one any has no hope. One little girl has.

And there is joy in her, that spontaneous, combustible urge I have seen so often in young creatures, so seldom among older, pleasure-seeking adults. I had been reading that evening about joy as Joseph Wood Krutch describes it in the lives of creatures other than man. He sees the robin's song as expressive of joy "real and instinctive." The robin's music does sound joyous, but the chorus singing the "Ode to Joy" in Beethoven's Ninth Symphony rivals it in joyous expression, yet many of them may be worrying about the rent. To me joy is that unpredictable moment when a calf, kicking up its heels for no perceptible reason, leaves friends and flies behind in a spurt of purposeless well-being. Or when Jeremy runs suddenly across the lawn, followed enthusiastically by Fernando, and rolls to a stop on her back. Jeremy, like the calf, feels those sudden injections of joy. As I say, I am not so sure about Dr. Krutch's robin. I cannot always recognize joy when I hear it, but when I see it bubble up in Jeremy and Corporal Salt, it makes me laugh.

Jeremy at that moment could choose her music, her friends, her path. And a world filled with animals was to her the best of all possible worlds. She had no need for signs proclaiming someone else's convictions. Hers were written in her open smile.

But she was being patient. It was time to eat, and she needed no cocktail ritual to prepare herself. She turned the pages of the thick book and waited.

"Let's eat, Stub."

"I was hoping you'd say that," she said, putting the book down.

She went to the kitchen to cook hamburgers and beans, our usual menu for nights at home, and I picked up the book she had been reading. It was an old book with torn dust jacket called *Common Sense Horsemanship*, a relic from my Connecticut days with Chestnut when I thought I could know a horse by reading about one. Jeremy had been reading a chapter with the commanding title "Imagine You Are a Horse." I began to read.

I knew how much Jeremy wanted a horse of her own and how tantalizing it was for her to come to the Valley with me those weekends where horses were all around us. On our trips to Solvang young girls rode their horses along the road. In every yard was a stand of horses, black and beige and copper beneath a walnut tree. Horse trailers, those Roman chariots of the West, rolled along the country roads, their open stalls revealing the fat, sleek rumps of more horses. For a girl who wanted a horse, the Valley was an irresistible place to be, but not to have one of her own must have been like standing outside the fence at Disneyland. She carried lumps of sugar from Mattei's in her pocket wherever she went, and she went to call on all horses near us. She knew their virtues. She did not ask me for a horse because she knew I wanted to buy her one. And now with my deductions out there grazing, walking my fence as if it were the Chisolm Trail, it was time. I settled farther down in my chair, put my feet up on another, and read.

Horse books are usually about as helpful to a prospective horse owner as books on gynecology would be to a prospective bridegroom. Impossible instructions, dire warnings, alarming symptoms fill their pages, together with diagrams, menus, rib counts, and diseases. They often start out by affirming that the horse was never built to be ridden at all, trace his ancestry from some five-toed, dog-sized animal to the present animal, a California status symbol outnumbered only by swimming pools and surfboards. They then remind us that our own ancestors ate horses and never dreamed of mounting one, but then our ancestors had no guns, so horses survived their first contact with people.

Horse books are more like new-car manuals than serious attempts to encourage an understanding of the animal. No writer of horse books really imagines he is on a horse. He simply reasons that a horse well fed, well groomed, well disciplined will behave less like a living creature and more like a new Chevrolet than a horse mistreated.

After placing the horse's mental capacities well below those of the dog, the cat, the elephant, and other animals, the horse expert confesses that horses don't like people. This fact is followed by a testimonial to the horse's excellent memory. Perhaps the horse remembers having his tail refashioned by the blue-ribbon winner, his genitals squeezed by the bucking strap of the rodeo rider, his nostrils slit by the marauding Indian. Perhaps now that he has learned to walk on one toe he wonders why people not only need five but a spur on each heel. If horses can see what is behind, as well as what is before them, they have a right to their dislike of us.

Horses, my books tell me, have no morals, and why should they? Morality, a human evaluation of right and wrong, as imposed upon animals by men who claim to know the difference, is hardly necessary equipment for a horse. Servitude and enforced obedience are the lot of horses. And instincts are more dependable than morals. No, I am not looking for a moral horse.

Horses, I am pleased to report, are ticklish. I have no idea where they are most ticklish, and see no reason to poke around under their elbows to find out, but somehow it's nice to know. Chestnut never giggled when I put the saddle on, but he did try to put his hoof in my mouth. I am pleased also to discover that horses have few worries, although as always I wonder how anyone ever determined this. Ulcers are not listed among horse diseases, and furrowed brows are rare, but the whinny of a mare separated from her foal, the struggles of a horse unable to get to this feet in a tight corner may indeed be signs of worry. They simply don't have *our* worries. Dandruff, yellowing teeth, and the inability to burp, all horse problems, are not worth the worry.

But I finished the chapter without once being able to imaging myself a horse. I imagined several times what I could do if I were a horse, but those were immoral thoughts. I closed the book and sniffed hamburgers sizzling in the kitchen.

"It says horses aren't very smart," I told Jeremy.

"I know," she said, "but they really are. Pancho knows me

already and we only just met last week. I think they know a lot."

"Would you take care of a horse?" I asked her. "You know, keep his feet clean and feed him?"

"Of course. That's easy."

"I'll call Farmer about it," I promised. "We really should have a horse."

Jeremy carried the plates to the table and sat down. "I think so too," she said. That's what I like - children who agree with me.

Jim Farmer has a cowboy's attitude toward horses. I doubt if he has ever read a horse book or even knows how many ribs they have. His horses roam free across his ranch in perfect health and as wild as mustangs, while he, a Montana cowboy, ventures out every spring to rope one and break it sufficiently for the *Ranchero* ride in May. Jeremy's riding experience began with children's pony rides and progressed as far as those supervised group excursions organized by Los Angeles stables on animals so old and broken in spirit they walk the same path day after day like carousel horses. My daughter's confidence outdistanced her ability as a rider, but Farmer would know a horse for her, so I called our friend.

"Just been down dippin' out some trout for breakfast," he said. Jim has a small trout pond so overstocked that the fish have to climb over each other to get from one end to the other. At each end a squad of angry ducks patrols the banks, as if to keep the trout from crawling out of the pond. He used the word "dippin'" advisedly.

"Jeremy wants a horse," I told him.

"Well, we'll find one for her. Matter of fact, I heard of a bay mare for sale. One of the girls at the Pancake House owns her. Stop in for coffee tomorrow."

I thanked him, hung up, and found Jeremy's nose very close.

"Did he have one?"

"A bay mare at the Pancake House," I told her.

"Really?" She laughed. "At the Pancake House? When can we see her?"

"Tomorrow, Stub. Now don't count on it. But we'll take a look."

We went to bed early, as always, dreams of bay mares about

83

to overtake us. Fernando, who lets out a satisfied grunt whenever he lies down, like an old man settling into a rocking chair, signaled that he was through for the day, and the quiet country night moved in around us.

We drove to Farmer's office early Saturday morning, horses on our minds. Jim met us in his doorway dressed as usual in Western shirt, Ranchero belt buckle, and tight Western pants that make it almost impossible to put your hands in your pockets. Western clothes are designed for tall, thin men like Jimmy Stewart. Fatter ones, like me, must squeeze into the same clothes and be satisfied to bulge a little and take no deep breaths.

"Let's go have coffee," Jim suggested.

My ranching friends were lined up as usual on the short stools, sipping coffee and exchanging wisdom. They made room for us, and Jeremy ordered pastry and waited for the horse talk to begin. A pretty woman in a Danish costume brought out orders, and Farmer asked her about the horse.

"Yes, we're selling the mare. She's eight years old, part Appaloosa and part Arabian. Nice little mare. Want to see her?"

"Oh, I know that horse," Jim said. "You know her, Ed."

Ed and several others nodded. They all knew the horse. They all know every horse in the Valley, although when they have a chance to meet them all I can't imagine, unless the horses come in for coffee.

"My husband's over at the corral now," the woman, whose name was Mrs. Santangelo, a nice Danish name, told us. "I'll call him to tell him you'll be by."

We thanked her and left with directions to the horse. Farmer went back to his office, while Jeremy and I drove off down the road to Buellton.

"Is eight too old?" she asked me.

"Eight is just right. That would make her twenty-eight if she were human."

On a spur off the freeway Jeremy and I came upon the old barn and corral crowded with hungry cattle where the horse was supposed to live. And she was there, aloof in a corner of bare ground, appearing to be lonesome. Mr. Santangelo, a gray-haired giant, met us and invited us to climb the fence and meet "Dee."

"Her name is Deyos Princess Tammy," he explained. "We just call her Dee."

Jeremy was over the fence and at Dee's side while I still struggled at the top of the rail, but I decided to make it look deliberate. I had read lists of instructions to the prospective horse buyer, and I was trying to remember a few things. I walked up to the horse - small for a horse, I thought - and felt her nose, which was warm and soft. Her brown eyes - large for a horse, I thought - were deep and gentle. I bared her teeth (mares have thirty-six, I remembered) and noticed that they were yellowish and large and that being forced to smile changed her whole expression, so I lowered her lip and nodded wisely. I walked around her, noticing how round she was, then ran my hand down her leg, which felt lumpy but no worse than my own. I nodded again to Jeremy. I noticed that she had white patches on her hind legs. On one side the white came only a few inches above her hoof, while her other hind leg was white half way up her leg. I tried to lift her hoof to examine it, but she kept it firmly on the ground. I frowned at Jeremy. Obviously she was hiding something. Santangelo walked over and lifted the hoof for me to examine, so I peered at it. It looked healthy to me, so I nodded to Jeremy. My examination was complete.

"Seems to be in good shape," I announced.

"She's just been wormed," Santangelo said.

"I meant to ask you about that," I told him. "Can't be too careful."

Santangelo threw a heavy Western saddle on Dee's back, slipped the bridle on and invited Jeremy to try her out. Dee marched around the corral under Jeremy as calmly as any horse she had ridden, and her smile, Jeremy's that is, was enough to convince me.

"What are you asking?"

"Oh, I'll take three hundred. Throw in the saddle and bridle for an extra fifty. I even got a paper on her."

"Can we get her, Daddy?" Jeremy asked from the saddle.

"You sure you like her?" I always ask foolish questions.

"I love her."

"Okay. We'll take her."

Dee's arrival that afternoon in Santangelo's trailer changed our status, at least in my estimation, and gave the ranch a new dimension. Her first droppings landed on the driveway, a badge of honor. A new and delightful smell had been added to the Townsend ranch, manure mixed with saddle leather, to blend with the wonderful smells I had collected so far. The breath of a steer is a warm-milk smell, sweet and clean. The hay bale is the smell of summer, packaged for sniffing all year round. The pasture, watered and green, is a wet smell of plants and animals combined. Dee's new mixture added to the subtlety of perfume around us.

Dee's first day with us was exciting. Jeremy tried out the combs and brushes we had bought in town until Dee shone like a parading Thoroughbred. She sat for minutes on Dee's back while the horse blinked peacefully in the sunshine. I leaned over the corral rail like the Virginian and scratched my lean-muscled jaw.

Dee's certificate from the Appaloosa Horse Club, with its gold seal, testified to her birth in February, 1961, in Riverside, California, sired by Peacock's Prince, out of Anglo Arab. On her sire's side she was Appaloosa, while her dam was half Arabian and half Thoroughbred. A very distinguished horse, we thought, already a member of the club and with a noble-sounding ancestry. I put the certificate on the mantle for all to see.

Late that afternoon we let her out into the pasture and together our black steers and bay mare completed the furnishing of our field. At dinner Jeremy praised Dee's gentleness, and I put the horse book back on the shelf. Dee suited my daughter and suited me. Her one white stocking and one sock did look as if she had dressed in the dark, but if that didn't bother her, it certainly wouldn't bother me.

"And she just met Pancho across the fence," Jeremy told me. "I think they're going to be friends when we aren't here."

The following weekend Jeremy plunged into horse care with abandon. She began by giving Dee her first shampoo, using a tube of Prell and a garden hose and causing the horse to turn into a high cloud of lather that would have warmed the heart of any soap company. When it was all over, Dee rolled violently in the dirt of the corral, while Jeremy stood by helplessly. I bought cans of fly spray and bottles of blue liquid for her scratches. The tack room began to fill up with blankets and saddle soap, ropes and bridles, hoof picks and tail combs. Dee suffered all this attention without complaint, but when Jeremy opened the corral gate, she took off at full gallop to the far end of the field, where Pancho waited under the oak tree. There the two horses stood nose to nose across the barbed-wire fence being, I suppose, gregarious. But I was wrong. Dee, for God's sake, was madly in love.

By the third week of Dee's residence the love affair between her and Colonel Pomfit's old gelding was in full flower. "Flower" may not quite be the word, for my fence separated everything except their noses, and a gelding, as everyone except Dee knows, has very little to offer a mooning mare. But what Pancho lacked in capacity he compensated for in noise. Using every form of cajolery from oats to apples Jeremy would drag Dee down the field to the corral, while Pancho whinnied shrilly from the fence like an old man at a burlesque show. Both horses called back and forth to each other all day from opposite ends of the field, and no amount of explanation from Jeremy seemed to convince Dee that Pancho was a poop as a lover.

Jeremy saddled Dee and tried to ride her up the road, but she never got past Pancho. Dee would back and fill and refuse all orders as the two horses came abreast of each other across the fences, and Jeremy's riding skill was limited. Our stately Appaloosa with the gentle eyes and nuzzling nose had become a frantic romantic, eyes ablaze, nose all scratched up, all for the love of a cow horse old enough to be her father. Something had to be done.

"I think we should get her a mascot," Jeremy suggested after watching Dee break every track record in her dash back to Pancho. "Horses like a goat for company."

"I don't think Dee wants a goat," I answered.

"But, Daddy, it would calm her nerves."

I decided to calm my own instead and went to dress for dinner.

Betty McClelland, one of the owners of Mattei's Tavern, met us as we arrived. "How's the horse?" she asked.

"She's in love," I told her.

"We may have to get a goat," Jeremy added.

Betty looked puzzled, so I explained Jeremy's theory of calming a mare in heat by providing a goat for distraction.

"If you think it'll work, I know where you can get a goat," she said.

"Do you think it'll work?" I asked her.

She laughed. "We'll, it wouldn't work for me, but then I'm not a horse."

"Neither is a goat."

"But strange things happen around here," she said. "And I know where you can get a goat."

"I don't want to know, Betty."

The following Saturday Dee seemed calmer. Perhaps the first infatuation was over and her relationship with Pancho, separated from her by the fence, had reached the "let's-be-sensible" stage. Pancho could be seen leaving Dee at the fence while he circled his corral for food, and now and then Dee would walk away from him just to show that she didn't need him either. But their desolate cries to each other when Dee was pulled down to our corral were still poignant, lovelorn of snorts.

Jeremy and I were eating lunch when our doorbell rang. At the door were Betty's two teenage daughters, each holding a small goat, one brown and one white, about the size and shape of bagpipes held upside down.

"Mother says the white one is for you," one of the girls announced and presented the small warm goat to Jeremy. The girl then handed me a nursing bottle and explained that the goat had to be fed every four hours with powdered milk and warm water.

Without waiting for any reaction from us the girls left, and we stood there holding goat and bottle.

"Isn't he cute, Daddy?"

"My God, he isn't even weaned yet. Put him down and see what happens."

The goat stood there, wobbling on long legs like a small boy trying out his first stilts. Its body, somewhat concave, swayed gently, its ears, pink scoops, wiggled back and forth above two black horn sprouts. Its eyes, black horizontal pupils set in white irises, were solemn, its nose was pink, and its wide, thin-lipped mouth was turned up at the corners, giving it an expression of mild disbelief. I didn't blame it. I didn't believe it either. Suddenly its mouth opened, a red tongue shot straight out like one of those paper horns people blow at parties, and it let out a high-pitched squawk like a boy's first note on a saxophone. Jeremy picked it up again, and immediately the squawk stopped and the goat tucked its nose under her chin. I stuck the nipple into the side of its mouth like a cigar, and the goat began to suck.

"Let's take him out to see Dee," Jeremy suggested.

"No, Stub," I said. "He won't stay there, and he'll give the horse a nervous breakdown."

But we tried it. Dee nosed the goat briefly and then walked to the fence to call Pancho. The goat let out another shriek, Fernando barked, and Jeremy carried Dee's companion back to the house.

Why do I do these things? I've been doing it for years, each time learning my lesson, always forgetting again that my house is not the Ark. My wife is no help. She confidently believes she will return in the next life as an otter and plans to get one so that she can get some instruction before the time comes. Nicole keeps a kangaroo rat in her bedroom, and on countless occasions the cry "The rat's out" sends the household into chaos. Beds and chairs are moved, doors slammed before the cats can beat us to the rat, and the search goes on. Susie's dog Hari is the only dog I ever knew that can scratch and eat at the same time. Of course, if he hadn't learned to do this he would have starved to death. Jeremy likes to bring home free kittens. Now a baby goat.

"I better buy some powdered milk," I said. "You heat the water."

"And get another nipple, Daddy. Simon ate this one."

"Simon?"

"His name is Simon Capri. Look! He thinks I'm his mother."

By bedtime several important facts had been established about our goat. The first was that he needed a companion far more than Dee and would not be left alone. Wherever we went, he followed on noiseless hooves, sitting on our laps when we sat, keeping us always in sight. The second fact was that Simon's appetite was renewed each hour, and a warm bottle stuck in the side of his face was the only alternative to an air raid alarm all night long. The third fact, which I've always known but seldom admitted, is that it is impossible to housebreak a goat. He did have the courtesy to raise his tail like a warning flag on a battleship just before opening fire, but Jeremy's room was a shambles by morning. And Simon could look me right in the eye through it all, even if he did it sideways.

There was nothing to do but take the goat with us when we left on Sunday for Los Angeles. Simon enjoyed the ride and seemed to enjoy watching my whole family carpeting the house with newspapers when we arrived. Bottles were heated, cats scattered in terror, and a neighbor called to ask if we had a new baby. Simon sat in any available lap, slept in any occupied bed, and when put outside, sent his siren cry echoing across Pacific Palisades. After two days I called Betty and told her the goat was not working out very well. Even my children accepted my verdict. By now they were red-eyed from lack of sleep, their school clothes spotted with milk, and Simon had eaten the end off the rat's tail. They all decided to go to the ranch with me to find a new home for him.

Giving away a goat is difficult, as we had learned in Connecticut. Giving one back is more difficult. But Betty had promised to try, and I called her from the ranch, trying to muffle the goat long enough to speak to her.

"I found somebody," she told me. "But it wasn't easy."

The "somebody" turned out to be a woman in Buellton, so on

a Saturday morning we all headed sadly for Buellton. Simon sat happily on Jeremy's lap, wearing his new collar and leash, nibbling raisin branflakes out of a bowl and being a very well-behaved goat. The address in Buellton turned out to be a store front, a sort of lunchroom with a Mexican name and no customers.

"It's a restaurant," Nicole cried.

"Oh, no," wailed Susie. "Daddy, you wouldn't leave him at a restaurant."

"Nothing better than goat enchiladas," I said and left them in the car while I hunted for Simon's new owner. A man sat at the counter sipping coffee and a young girl washed dishes across the counter from him.

"Are you expecting a goat?" I asked.

The man looked up at the girl. "Did she say she'd take that goat?"

"Damn!" the man shouted, setting his cup down hard on the counter. "I guess she did. Wait here a minute."

"It's a pet, you know," I reminded him.

He grinned then. "You think I'd eat goat?" he snorted and walked out the door.

By the time I had reassured the girls and patted the goat, the man came back around the store with his wife. "Don't worry about your goat," she told the girls. "We have a ranch up the road. He'll have lots of company." She noticed the long faces in the car window and smiled. "I promise," she added.

Slowly Jeremy opened the door and lifted Simon Capri to the ground. He stood wagging his tail and smiling his thin-lipped little smile while the woman took the leash from Jeremy.

"His name is Simon," she told the woman. Then she gave her the bottle and waved at Simon, but he had already found a tuft of new grass and was nibbling as we drove away.

"Do you think he'll remember us when we visit him?" Jeremy asked, a tear rolling slowly down her cheek.

I said I felt sure he would.

At eleven-fifteen on Saturday morning, the eighth day of June, our telephone rang. The event was so unusual that Fernando barked and even Corporal Salt stood up and peered through the fence near the house. Jeremy was out in the corral attempting to make Dee jump over a small pile of hay, while I sat inside the house looking at the grass and wondering if I would have to mow it. We don't get many calls. In fact, our average is about one a month, and the ring usually upsets everybody, but I didn't take this lack of interest in us as anything to brood about. I do check now and then with the Solvang operator to make sure the telephone still works, and she rings me back to prove it does, and, of course, there are my Sunday morning calls to Freddie and the girls, just to let them know that I am too tired to do any gardening when Jeremy and I get home. Nielson Downs called in May to ask how the steers were doing, which was neighborly, and only a few weeks ago a small boy knocked at our front door and asked me if my mother was home. He was selling Christmas cards. But now the phone was ringing.

"Townsend?" the caller barked.

I agreed.

"This is Colonel Pomfit," the authoritative voice announced. "We're moving to Florida and I wondered if you wanted to buy my horse."

I sighed.

"I've noticed how your mare gets along with Pancho. Of course, I have other buyers, but I decided to ask you first. I'm making up a package including Pancho, a power mower, and my pickup. Eight hundred for the lot."

"I have a lawnmower," I said weakly.

"Have to get out July first. Want to move it all. Let me know."

I almost saluted. Pomfit has that effect on people. "I will, sir," I promised. "I'll have to discuss it with my daughter."

"Have her come over and see Pancho," Pomfit said.

"I'll let you know," I told him and hung up.

"Who called?" Jeremy asked.

"Colonel Pomfit," I told her. "He wants to sell Pancho."

"Why? Pancho must be valuable."

I explained the whole, complex proposal

"You could ride Pancho and I could ride Dee," Jeremy said, warming up like an electric heater. "And we need a truck."

"I better mow the lawn, Stub. It's grown while I've been sitting here."

7

*"Everything about my truck was made to last.
Its frame was heavy, the metal rigid, the engine big and
sturdy. Of course I treated it well..."*
- JOHN STEINBECK

After lunch Jeremy and Fernando and I walked up the long dirt road that runs beside our pasture, then on beyond our fence line until it reaches the paved road to Solvang. Pomfit's house, a sprawling, one-story ranch house similar to ours, lay off to the right on an acre of ground, most of which was Pancho's corral. The colonel was out cutting a patch of high grass with a scythe, and he looked healthy enough to be drafted. Pomfit, I suppose, was in his early fifties, a career officer with a gray military crewcut, squared shoulders, and a slim waist. he was the sort of man who would allow grass to grow a foot before cutting it so that he could use a scythe instead of a mower. I had learned from other neighbors that he had been a rodeo rider, pilot, surfer, and war hero. Now that he was moving to Florida I supposed he would add Jai Alai and roping alligators in the Everglades to his accomplishments, while I went on moving my pipes and breathing hard.

He saw us coming but went right on swinging his scythe until we were within a few feet of the long blade.

"Looks like hard work," I said, always one to open with a peppy little observation.

"Loosens the back muscles," Pomfit grunted. "Want to see the horse?"

He left the scythe leaning against the side of his house and led us around to the corral. While we stood at the gate, he grabbed the lead rope and strolled over to Pancho, who seemed much larger than I remembered him. Pomfit tossed the rope around the horse's neck, then leaped on his back and began to ride him in small circles, guiding him with the rope and his knees. The old horse responded without bit or saddle, doing his little dance there in the corral. Jeremy and I were impressed.

"Had him since he was a colt," Pomfit called to us. He jumped down and invited Jeremy to try him, this time slipping on the bridle, but still no saddle. He boosted Jeremy up and handed her the reins. "Use your knees and lean in the direction you want him to go," Pomfit told her. Jeremy used her knees and leaned, but the horse just stood there and leaned also. "Turn him with the reins, but don't pull hard," Pomfit ordered, but Pancho waited. The colonel grabbed the reins and immediately the horse plodded off with Jeremy perched on top of him like a small irritation.

"How old is he?" I asked.

"Seventeen. Right in his prime."

"Seems to be lame in his right foreleg," I observed shrewdly.

"Got caught in barbed wire. Favors it sometimes," Pomfit said.

"Is his saddle included?"

"Taking it to Florida," the colonel said. I remembered all those alligators waiting to be roped.

Jeremy slid down and walked over to us. The horse followed behind her and joined the conversation, his chin brushing Pomfit's head.

"He'd be good for you, Daddy," Jeremy said. "He's very gentle."

"I can see that, Stub. I could bring along a book and relax."

"Oh, he'll go," Pomfit assured us.

"Can I take a look at the pickup, Colonel?"

"It's right behind the garage. My wife has geraniums planted in it now, but we'll take those out. It's a nice little forty-seven Chevy."

And there behind the garage, in grass up to its running boards, was Pomfit's truck, a battleship-gray pickup resting on half-filled tires and resplendent with flowers. Mrs. Pomfit had turned its bed into a garden, which told me something about her and the truck, but I must say it was gaudy.

"This may be a collector's item," Pomfit explained as he led us to the pickup.

"I'm not a collector," I told the colonel. "Does it run?"

"It was running like a top before my wife decided to plant it."

Remembering how tops ran, I asked him to start it. He fumbled through a cookie jar filled with old keys until he found one he liked and jumped into the cab, while the truck sank lower into the grass. Needless to say, it wouldn't start. In fact, it wouldn't even try.

"Battery's dead," Pomfit grunted. "Tell you what, I'll tune her up later and bring her down for you to try."

"I was thinking of buying a newer model," I protested.

"Trucks never change. Just going to use it to go to the dump, aren't you?"

"Well, I had planned to come back in it too."

He barked once and straightened his shoulders. "How about the mower?"

"I have a mower."

"Never hurts to have two."

"Let me think about it Colonel," I told him, hoping to escape. I was beginning to be afraid I might end up buying anything he offered and enlisting in the Army as well if we didn't get out of there.

"I'll call you," I added.

"Okay, Townsend, but don't wait too long. Gotta move this

stuff out. And remember," he said, giving me a nasty jab in the ribs, "the best thing for the inside of a man is the outside of a horse."

Oh, well. Jeremy and I walked back down the road. She was convinced by now that Pancho at any price should be snapped up, I that the whole thing was ridiculous. Later in the afternoon we saw a large cloud of black smoke rising from Pomfit's garage, so I suppose he must have gotten the truck started, but he never arrived in it. Maybe all those geraniums were just too much of a load.

Before Jeremy and I set out for dinner at Mattei's I reached my decision and called Pomfit. His wife answered.

"Would you tell your husband," I said, "that I'll pay a hundred dollars for Pancho, but I've decided I don't want the truck."

She agreed to relay the message. "But I don't think he wants to sell separately. He thinks of it as a package, you know."

"I know," I said, and hung up.

"Do you think he'll sell just Pancho?" Jeremy asked.

"I doubt it, but we'll see. The horse won't go, and neither will the truck, so unless he plans to hitch them both to his mower I don't see how he is going to move anything out."

But the weekend went by, and then the week, with no call from Pomfit.

The following weekend, while we were waiting in vain to hear from Pomfit, and Pancho and Dee were still nose to nose in love, I was invited to a barbecue. But this was no suburban excuse for cooking in the backyard. This was my first Western barbecue, given by a couple of local ranch hands who owned a cabin high in the Santa Ynez Mountains east of Lake Cachuma, for all their friends rugged enough to survive it. I was included at the last minute by Bud New, the owner of Mattei's Tavern, who must have guessed that I would enjoy this Early American Drinking and Eating Contest, but who, I'm sure, did not guess that the mountain melee would lead to my buying a truck. But then, neither did I when I set out in my aging Cadillac at six that Saturday night to find the barbecue.

Leaving Jeremy and a girl friend behind at the ranch, I drove

97

out across the Valley while there was still plenty of light and had no difficulty finding the road leading past the Ranger Station beyond the lake. I was just beginning to feel like a cowboy on his way to town after a long trail drive when I came to the Santa Ynez River, a bubbling stream feeding the lake, then, beyond the lake, making its was across the Valley to the sea. But at this particular spot the river crossed the road. By that I mean that the road sloped down under the river and up again on the other side. No wagon master worth his salt block would balk at this minor hazard, but I had never crossed a river before by driving through it. I stopped, thinking of cattle and horses fording the stream, their noses just above the water, and wondered how deep it was. I was on the right road, others had obviously made the crossing, and this was the West. After all, if I had to cross rivers on bridges I should have stayed in Connecticut. I said a few encouraging words to my car and plunged in.

The river bottom was firm, the water only deep enough to flow under the car doors, and the Cadillac's blue nose was well out of the water and making good headway until I reached the opposite bank. There I hit ground rather suddenly and felt something beneath my car give way. I crawled slowly over the bank and along the road again, dragging part of the car behind me. I stopped, looked under the car and saw that the tailpipe and a few other entrails were hanging down, but the engine purred, and I was safely across, so I continued over the deteriorating road up into the mountain where, the barbecue was to be held. By the time I found the cabin, surrounded by pickups, it was growing dark, and the crowd was there. In the clearing, lit dimly by two naked bulbs hanging from a loose wire strung from the cabin, were about fifty people. They were clustered at an open fire where corn was piled, roasting Indian style in the husks, while near by was a long picnic table almost completely covered by the cooked carcass of a large pig. Off to one side was a smaller table covered with bottles, and the party was well started. A drink in a paper cup was placed in my hand, followed by another drink in a paper cup for the other hand. One man hacked chips of ice from a huge block with a small hatchet, another stirred a pot of beans the size of a nose cone, and there were enough whoops and "hot damns" to fill the night air for a mile around.

I was passed from group to group, shaking calloused hands and getting pounded on the back, balancing my drinks and wincing over vicelike grips. The men wore dusty boots and Levis, warm sheepskin jackets, and Western hats. The women wore dusty boots and Levis, warm sheepskin jackets, and Western hats. But their hands were smaller, although just as hard, so I was able to tell when I was shaking hands with a girl. It was explained to all, of course, that I was the new owner of the Small ranch.

Then came dinner. We were handed paper plates and plastic bowls and invited to fend for ourselves. We hacked chunks of steaming pork from the mountain of meat on the table, filled our bowls with beans from the gigantic pot, and peeled the husks from the corn ears, painting butter on with a huge paint brush. And there, standing in the clearing, with drinks perched on rocks and platefuls of wild pig, we ate. By now my boots were dusty, my fingers greasy, my devotion to this Western feast complete. Never had food tasted so good. Never had companions seemed so hospitable. Never had a napkin and a chair seemed so unnecessary.

And then the games began. A truck was backed into the clearing and a portable radio installed on its tailgate. Music, loud and Western, blared into the crowd, and couples began to dance, kicking up small dust clouds, clutching each other in strong arms, belt buckle to belt buckle. But that was not all. Two swarthy cowboys grabbed a lariat and invited one and all to skip rope. There in the moonlight one grizzled cowboy after another took his turn hopping over the revolving rope, laughing, tripping, and staggering off to the bar for refreshment. The evening's casualty came when one weathered gunfighter got his heel caught in the twisting rope, fell heavily, and broke his ankle. I suppose I came West too late. When the fastest gun in the Santa Ynez Mountains has to be carried away on a stretcher, not after a shoot-out or taking his turn on a wild mustang, but because he tripped while jumping rope, it is enough to shake the convictions of a lifetime. I withdrew before they decided to play hide and seek.

My trip back was uneventful. Dragging the bowels of my Cadillac over the mountain road and plowing across the river again, I regained the highway. But I resolved to buy a pickup and join my neighbors as a full-fledged member of a society where a truck is a social, as well as a professional necessity.

I decided to shop for a truck in Los Angeles because there are more of them there, parked in the rear of new-car showrooms, out of sight, but available on demand. As I went from Ford to Chevrolet to Dodge, I discovered that the usually ebullient Los Angeles salesman is less than overwhelmed by a potential truck buyer. He strides toward you, golf tanned and smiling his little welcome to easy payments, but the smile fades, the tan pales when he discovers that all you want is a pickup. And I soon discovered why. There is little profit to the dealer or his salesman in pickups, unless you agree to add all sorts of extras. I rejected carpeting, air conditioning, power transmission, spotlights, and tool kits, leaving only the stripped lonesome truck itself, and at last settled on a new, blue Chevy pickup whose only luxuries were a radio and a rear bumper with a knob on it for a horse trailer.

A schizophrenic problem quickly threatens new truck owners. It began for me with the less-than-arm-twisting persuasion from the salesman. Then, as I drove it out of the lot, feelings of inferiority quickly turned to the glow of Olympian superiority when from the cab I looked down upon the rest of the motoring world around me. I rode above them all, bounding along above the roofs of ordinary cars with a clear view of the horizon, like a pilot who suddenly leaves the earth behind. This dichotomy, or truckdriver's dilemma, continued as I drove my new truck around Los Angeles that first week. I left it for the doorman to park at the Beverly Hills Hotel and was blinded by his distaste, fully expecting to be sent around to the service entrance for my luncheon appointment. At one restaurant a sneering attendant simply told me where to park and left me to my own devices.

But I also discovered a new society of which I was now a

100

member. Young men with unrealized dreams of the open road, reinforced, perhaps, by memories of a Middlewest farm, admired my truck and waved from motorcycles, welcoming me to the club. Parked among the Cadillacs and Lincolns it towered proudly over them, while their owners seemed to envy the implicit freedom from economic competition my truck represented. I was not a gardener, for there were no rakes or lawnmower handles hanging from the tailgate, so I must be a man who has spurned upholstery and high payments for life's more lasting values. I felt superior again, and I noticed that drivers around me on Los Angeles streets gave me wide berth. I was impregnable, they assumed, like a tank, and so I drove down Wilshire Boulevard gunning my six-cylinder engine and scattering Rolls Royces like terrified chickens.

After a week of introducing Los Angeles to my truck Jeremy and I left for the ranch in it. She and Fernando rode in the back, where Jeremy stretched out on an old mattress and Fernando stood guard, barking at motorcycles and wagging at policemen all the way to the Valley. There we began a new and much easier life. I immediately filled the truck on Saturday morning with all the accumulated rubbish I could find and headed for the dump, where I was congratulated by one and all on my purchase. The superintendent of the dump climbed aboard to help me shovel the load out, after which we all stood around comparing trucks for a while. I resolved to scrape up a load every week now that I had the truck, for at least at the dump I was no longer "the new owner of the Small ranch," but "the owner of that blue pickup with the collie." Fernando rode majestically in the wind wherever I went, and in front of the Pancake House my truck nestled comfortably among the others. Jeremy mentioned something about buying a horse trailer so that we could haul Dee back and forth with us, but for the time being I ignored her. For a man who less than two years ago had never felt the wet leather of a steer's nose, I was doing pretty well. My herd, my horse, and my truck were all there to prove it.

8

*"Our coach was a great swinging and swaying stage,
of the most sumptous description -
an imposing cradle on wheels."*
- MARK TWAIN

The end of June and the beginning of a second summer in the Valley. A transition time between green and gold, wet and dry, growth and maturity, when morning fog lingers a moment after sunrise as a final encouragement to growing plants to hold out under the persistent sun of summer. A time when animals too must face long hours of daylight heat, their coats thinned to a shining glaze, prey again for flies that seem to come, like guided missiles, straight out of June to the hot July backs of cattle and horses. The lawn at the ranch on such a morning is too wet to mow, yet by afternoon it is too dry to grow another day. The white birches are by now fully dressed, their anklet of jonquils gone for another spring, and my persistent gopher, preferring roots to tops, travels the low road. In full-blown field the six steers float like fat, black boats, their tassle tails swinging up over their backs, and Dee, standing taller and apart, chooses her own green breakfast. How well a horse has been measured! With knees straight he can brush the turf with his exploring nose. The error of an inch in his blueprint would force him to stoop for breakfast.

The end of June and the beginning of the summer vacation for my children. I decided to ask my whole family to join me at the ranch for a week or two. I had never seen it on a Wednesday or even a Monday. We could have a day without a pipe to move, a weed to pull, and in the new truck we could search out the far corners of the Valley, plunge into the church-supper circuit, and stop at all of the places I had been passing for so many months.

"What would you really like to do at the ranch this summer?" I asked.

"Go to San Francisco," Nicole announced.

"Go on a camping trip," said Jeremy.

"Yes, sleep in a trailer and eat out every night," Susie added.

"I used to pack into the High Sierras," Freddie added, referring to her day with an old boyfriend who might have been Kit Carson. At least, he certainly was all man.

I shuddered and went to sit down. How could they all decide to migrate just when I had collected six steers and a horse and a pickup, seven comfortable beds, four chairs, and a dishwasher? It was too late to go West. We were already there. And I had a horror of camping out. How could they reject the Small ranch for a Townsend U-Haul, a traveling aluminum cell?

"But Daddy, we want to go somewhere," Nicole insisted.

"Don't you want to see how the pioneers did it?" Susie asked me.

"You can rent one of those mobile homes," Freddie told us.

"But this is ridiculous. Here we have a beautiful ranch and an irrigated pasture and our own brand." I was shouting now. "I just bought a truck and fixed the garbage disposal. I don't want to cook on hot rocks and sleep in trailer parks and pitch horseshoes with strangers."

"And we could live in a trailer to save money so that we could spend one night in a hotel," Nicole continued.

"And we could fish," Jeremy said.

"And we could take Hari," Susie said, never allowing her favorite dog to be left out of things.

Restless nomadic little creeps! I agreed to investigate a rented mobile home.

Feeling somewhat like a cowboy star who has just had his television series canceled, I set about the job of locating a means of leaving the ranch just at the time when I wanted to be there most. A series of phone calls, beginning with a friend who knew somebody who knew where to rent what was described as a "motor home," led me to an alley in the San Fernando Valley stuffed with huge vehicles the size and shape of buses, and it was there, after more phone calls, that I reserved one of them for a week. I was taken on a tour of inspection by a small, crescent-shaped man who had apparently spent his life in one of these modern prairie schooners, but who still had difficulty locating most of its "conveniences." There was room for five people to sleep, provided of course, that the five people were small, malformed insomniacs who like to curl up on tabletops. There was a shower, where a trickle of bluish water drained down from the ceiling into the toilet bowl, and a refrigerator which, the man explained, did not work if the motor home was tilted. Generator, air conditioners, gas heater, water pump, tape deck, and fire extinguisher completed the equipment I saw that day. It was all immediately available.

I signed the contract and was given a pamphlet with a list of dumping stations to keep for my very own. I did not ask then what a dumping station was. I announced the arrangements at home that night and wondered again what was wrong with my family. Lewis and Clark and Admiral Byrd and Cortez probably came from broken homes, but I owned a ranch. What was I doing leaving it? How could I face Corporal Salt and Dee? How could I make them understand?

To make matters worse, Pancho was gone, and Dee stood at the fence, staring wistfully at his empty corral hour after hour, reluctant to even turn away for fear of missing a glimpse of him. A dog lying across his master's grave, Keats's "sick eagle looking at the sky," could not be more heartrending than the sight of Deyos Princess Tammy waiting for an old, lame horse that would never return. I should have bought Pomfit's truck. More foolish things have been done in the name of love.

I was to pick up the motor home Sunday on my return from the ranch, but on Saturday night Freddie called to tell me that my motor home had been rushed to Glen Campbell somewhere in Arizona. His, it seemed, had broken down..."by the time he got to Phoenix"...ha ha ha.

"Well," I said, "that's that. I always did like Glen Campbell."

"But they're getting us another one," Freddie assured me. "They're borrowing it from some man in Santa Monica."

"Well," I said, "that's that. I'll pick it up tomorrow night."

I said good-bye to Dee and the steers that Sunday morning and headed for Los Angeles. My first look at our new motor home the same evening was one of those optical flashes that remain forever filed in whatever file is kept for nightmarish visions. A huge white bus was parked in the alley with a broad red stripe around its middle. Black decals of spiders, three feet in diameter, and frighteningly realistic, were pasted across the rear and sides. Apparently it was owned by a traveling witch doctor, temporarily residing in Santa Monica while he brewed up new potions. I am not one for pasting signs on cars, although I did consider a bumper sticker that urged "Help Stamp Out Cattle Rustling" on my truck. Those spiders were fearsome.

Good sport that I am, I allowed myself to be taken on another guided tour of the bus, this time paying careful attention to master switches, water tanks, pump primers, and such, but I have never taken must interest in things I cannot cope with, and all I could think of was those damned spiders crawling up the sides of the vehicle. There was nothing to do but climb in the driver's seat and roll off down the road, doing my best to ignore the terrified faces of passing motorists, trying to get used to driving a huge bus. At the first red light I slammed on the brakes too suddenly, and most of the equipment came at me in a series of crashes. Ice trays, dishes, seat cushions tumbled around me, but I pressed on. There is a knack to driving a house on a freeway. I had to learn it.

We packed the bus that evening, filling every free space with clothes and food. A few neighbors watched from behind their curtains, but nobody dared come outside while that ghastly hulk was parked in front of my house.

"I forgot to ask what you dump at dumping stations," I said.

"Can't you imagine?" Freddie asked.

We would start off in the morning. The thrill of the unknown, which has propelled so many men in the past, is simply not for me. The prospect of driving that monster, even with my whole family riding shotgun beside me, curled my toes. I tried to look forward to the following Saturday when we would arrive, spiders and all, at the ranch, but the days between loomed dark indeed.

9

*"In America, there are two classes of travel -
first class, and with children."*
- ROBERT BENCHLEY

We packed ourselves and Hari into our motor home early Monday morning. Breakfast eaten, doors locked, cats and rat and Fernando arranged for, it was time to set the giant bus in motion. I sat in the driver's seat with a commanding view of the world around me, perched so high that I felt dizzy every time I looked down at the road beneath.

"Let's roll," I urged, like Ward Bond herding a bunch of Boston schoolteachers into Indian territory.

"Where are we going the first day?" somebody in back asked.

"Your mother's the camper. Ask her."

"I thought the High Sierra would be nice tonight," Freddie offered.

I sighed and started the bus. It would be foolish to protest now. We drove through town breaking off the branches of several trees and carrying them along with us, caught in the roof ventilators. As before, people in cars beneath us stared and pointed at the spiders, but the girls were busy pumping water, trying out the tape deck, and staggering up the aisle to the closet bathroom. At least this would be one trip where I would not have to stop every few miles for a gas-station ladies' room. And I was learning how to stop the bus without dislodging everything that was not nailed down. By applying the brakes a hundred yards before each traffic light I could grind to a halt with no more than a mild jerk. Susie's wheelchair rolled up and down the aisle each time, but at least the contents of the refrigerator remained in place.

We found the freeway and headed north toward the Mojave Desert, pushing along like a great white birthday cake under attack by giant insects. Going uphill the bus strained to make thirty miles an hour, but we came barreling down hills at an unstoppable sixty, terrifying Volkswagons all the way. I had noticed that the gas gauge was not working, the needle remained at half full, so I decided to stop in Palmdale to fill the tank. There were two tanks, one for gas and one for water, and I didn't know which was which, but the attendant smelled them both and decided on a place under the rear license plate. I remember that the gas bill was eleven dollars. The reason I remember this interesting detail is that every time we stopped the gas bill was eleven dollars. It is a curiously depressing sidelight.

As we drove through the foothills toward the town of Mojave and the edge of the great desert, music filled the bus. Simon and Garfunkel and Hari sang, Jeremy and Nicole and Susie sat at the dining room table asking about lunch, and Freddie rested on a rear bed, a high curving shelf where anyone shaped like a banana and only slightly larger could relax in perfect comfort. I was still in partial control of the bus from my driver's stool, but I was quickly developing an embarrassing and painful problem. I seemed to be developing hemorrhoids, and we were barely a hundred miles from Los Angeles. I plunged on toward the low-lying shacks of Mojave, determined to make it, but by the time we turned down the main street of that less than bustling town, I was, as they say, riding tall in the saddle.

We rolled to a stop on a side street in Mojave, close to a drug store and a Coke machine, which seemed to satisfy the immediate needs of the passengers and crew. Parked in that Western alley we also decided to try out the air conditioning system, our wind machine, located amidships in the bus and requiring the use of the generator. There was nothing to do except snap two switches, one located at the back of a closet crammed with clothes, the other located under the rear bunk. Anybody with an arm five feet long and a flashlight could easily manage that maneuver, and within minutes the generator was humming, a giant power plant sending kilowatts of energy all over the bus. The air conditioner seemed to respond nicely also, and a refreshing blast of air swept down the aisle. We were ready to enter the desert.

I have driven many times across this Western wasteland along the black strip of highway fringed with beer cans and stretching to a hump of horizon thirty miles distant. It is a place to admire at full speed, not a place to dally, but we decided to stop for lunch at a desolate turnoff where I could pull the bus into the sand. There we ate sandwiches and sipped cold drinks in the gusts from the air conditioner. I was beginning to feel less antagonistic toward to motor home and I relaxed and thumbed through my book of dumping stations, while Nicole watched for kangaroo rats to add to her collection of one. It was a peaceful siesta, one of the few I remember.

With nearly two hundred miles of desert between us and the Sierra it was time to push on, so we turned on the cool air and headed up the road. Our bus had two thermometers, one for outside temperature and one for inside. The outside one indicated 120 degrees in the early afternoon sun. The inside one showed a mere 90, but it was rising. Nicole kept me posted on the thermometers, calling out readings every few miles until outside of Bishop the two finally matched. Both were at the 120-degree mark, the top of the glass tube, ready, I suppose, to burst and continue rising up the side of the bus. At this point, with thermometers in a dead heat, I stopped and turned off the air conditioner, while everybody else flung the small windows open.

"At least it's a dry heat," we all told each other. All who ever crossed the desert have been saying that for a couple of centuries, as they perished of thirst on the salt flats. The *bon mot* ranks with those other comforting remarks like, "At least it went clean through" and "Somebody's bound to find us eventually."

We stopped for eleven dollars' worth of gas in Bishop and moved up the long winding road into the mountains. We were looking for a place to park the bus for the night, a quiet dell beside a bubbling trout stream and immediately adjacent to a well-stocked bar and steak house. The thermometers were plunging down again, Simon and Garfunkel and Hari were singing the latest hit, and I was wondering if it would be practical to drive standing up when we came to the Twin Lakes Ranger Station. Two signs were posted at the entrance: *Camping Allowed in Campsites Only* and *All Campsites Filled*. I pulled into the parking lot and stopped.

Inside the Ranger Station a girl dressed in a Smokey-the-Bear suit but without his endearing fuzzy face, greeted me and confirmed all campsites near the lake were filled. She did urge me to press on, however, and perhaps find an illegal spot for the bus. ("After all, who's going to find you tonight.") I agreed. We drove the bus further up into the mountains until my altimeter (yes, Mark Twain, my stage had an altimeter) registered ten thousand feet above sea level. There we came to the shore of one of the Twin Lakes, entirely surrounded by campers cooking their dinners in a small, blue cloud of smoke. Anyone lucky enough not to be driving a huge vehicle on a narrow curving road at twilight with no place to park it and no hope of dinner would have been struck by the scene. The small jewel lake, set at the foot of a towering snow-capped peak and fed by a white ribbon of waterfall cascading down from the snow, was beautiful, but I had come to the end of the road, and there was nothing to do but drive through a general store made of logs or stop.

"Get out and ask somebody where we can park," I ordered and out they got.

After ten minutes back they came, laden with bundles and followed by a woman who was gesturing to me to move the bus.

Freddie explained that after selling her a quantity of post cards, sweat shirts, and fishing hats the woman proprietor had agreed to let us park next to the store for the night, provided that we were gone by the time the store opened in the morning. The woman was still waving, so with Nicole and Jeremy riding drag I backed and maneuvered the bus into a small space between a gas pump and some trash cans. I have seldom turned off an engine with greater relief.

It was the cocktail hour, so with my feet on the dashboard I had a drink while the girls changed for dinner, walked Hari, and returned to tell me that there was a restaurant down the mountain a few miles. I had no idea how turn turn the bus around, but desperation is the mother of invention, and we accomplished it. We found the Alpine dining room and once again drove the bus up a winding path to a perch even a chipmunk could not back out of, but there was steak, there was pie, there was hot coffee, and we all felt better. After dinner my assistants once again stood in the dark, shouting instructions while I backed blindly down the path. Then back to our campsite for the first night's sleep.

The procedure necessary to allow five people to go to sleep in a motor bus is difficult to describe. It begins with the uprooting of seats, already piled with suitcases, to make flat surfaces, while up and down the narrow aisle people push along carrying mattresses and pillows in opposite directions, stumbling over obstacles and dumping their loads on the heads of other people who are brushing their teeth in the sink. Bed making is also colorful. Sheets and blankets are unfurled in the small space available, then tucked under tabletops and purses and Hari. Finally, when all was settled, we groped through the dormitory to the tiny bathroom, where we learned that it is amusing to wash one hand while pumping the faucet with the other. The lights went out at last, and the breeze from the snowbanks seeped into our motor home. Outside the night was the darkest I can remember. Inside a clock ticked and there was a trickling noise from the refrigerator. One memorable day was over. Only five remained.

I slept on a narrow cushion hanging from the ceiling of the

bus by two straps, sort of a bric-a-brac shelf for people, and awoke to the sound of knocking at the door. It was early and silent outside, but somebody, apparently, was up and eager.

I shinnied down the straps to the floor and opened the door. A man in a heavy jacket and wool cap stood outside, flanked by two small boys.

"You puttin' on a show tonight?" he asked, trying to peak into the bus.

I tried to pry my lips apart to answer, but it was too cold.

"I see the bus with the spiders pull in last night. My boys figured we'd like to see the show."

"No show. We're just camping," I mumbled.

"People here'd like a show," he persisted.

"We don't do anything," I told him.

"Sorry," he said and walked off, explaining to the boys that the circus had not come to Twin Lakes after all.

But I was up and the girls were stirring, so I decided to have breakfast. I started with the teakettle and after strenuous pumping got a trickle of water into it. We seemed to be low on water. I then opened the refrigerator and found where all the water was. The ice-cube trays had melted as had the sack of ice we had bought the day before at the gas station in Bishop. Obviously, the motor home refrigerator was not working. We had been tilted all night in the clearing, and, as promised, here soaking my feet was the result.

I dressed while the coffee water heated and went around to a trap door on the outside of the bus to find the primer for the gas heater. I found it, pumped it up and down, lit matches, and gave up. It was a silly thing to have attempted in the first place. I started the engine, hoping to warm up the bus for the others, and lit the other three burners on the stove. Then I sipped my coffee in silence while everybody else went up and down the aisle again, trailing blankets, hunting for clothes, and shivering. The first one up in a motor home has a big advantage. He can get out of the way.

An hour later, with the bedding stored, seats upright and the aisle cleared enough to see to the rear of the bus, we had breakfast and walked down to the lake shore. Fishermen were leaning patiently on the rail of a narrow bridge across a shallow inlet, the waterfall was tumbling down from the snows, and the crowded lake shore was alive with breakfast preparations. But we were not campers, we were squatters, and it was time to move before the ranger patrols came looking for us. We climbed back into the bus and headed out to the highway with a stop at Convict Lake next on our agenda.

The Sierra lakes, azure puddles of melted snow walled in by towering peaks, some snow-capped, others grizzled with pines, are the summer refuge of campers. The entrance to Convict Lake, like that to Twin Lakes, is a narrow, twisting road which comes to an abrupt end at just the wrong place. I remember it now only because again I had to back my clumsy bus out of the place, unable to see what was behind me. But it was a beautiful lake, according to my passengers, and we did escape without crushing any vacationers.

We headed north again to lunch at June Lake, where, unlike Convict Lake, there was a large town included and, miraculously, a large parking area at the far side of the lake for turning around. I pulled the bus into this clearing and stopped to calm my nerves near an abandoned picnic grounds, and while the girls and Hari went off to explore, and collect pine cones, I sat in the bus, sipping a can of beer, grateful for an hour or two of motionless peace. In fact, it was so quiet there in that empty parking lot at the edge of the forest that I sat, as I often do at the ranch, feet up, undisturbed by any sound, and stared at the crumbling picnic tables and a rusting Coca-Cola dispenser, all that was left of this particular unsuccessful human invasion.

And soon, at an opening in the metal box once filled with bottles and ice, there was a slight movement. A small head emerged, cautiously looking at the great white monster parked a few feet away, and, probably thinking it was only a large Coke container, a ground squirrel popped out. Then another followed, and another, until half a dozen small beige animals were cavorting around the clearing entering the Coke machine through one hole, exiting through another, chasing each other in and out of this tin fortress like children who have discovered an ancient castle.

113

I remember Loren Eiseley's comment: "It pays to know there is just as much future as there is past." It seemed to me as I sat there inside the bus that I was being offered a preview of that future when Nature has passed beyond the few human links in the chain of life and a subsequent society is evolving. The people were gone, leaving their Coke machines behind for ground squirrels to play tag in, and old dangers were forgotten. George M. Woodwell observed in the *Wall Street Journal*: "If man continues to degrade his land by dumping nutrients into the wrong places, we'll eventually kill off all species of fish, fowl, birds and animals we like, while the species we don't like will survive." He held out hope for crab grass, rats, crows, and inedible fish, "but eagles, pine trees and trout will disappear." But on that summer day at June Lake I felt more optimistic. While men still fished for trout across the lake, I was watching a colony of ground squirrels, shielded from the eagle by tall pines, having fun reclaiming their playground, improved, so far as they were concerned, by a vanished humanity. It didn't matter to them whether we liked them or not.

When my daughters returned, I eased the bus away and onto the road again and left the squirrels, perhaps momentarily frightened but soon reassured that the entire world had been returned to them.

Our trip north from June Lake was devoted to a search for a level patch of ground where we could park the motor home for the night, and in a deep canyon formed by the bubbling Walker River we found one. It was a spot at the edge of the river no larger than the bus, but there was room enough to back into it, and there was even a place for a campfire. While the girls sat on the riverbank watching for trout, I decided on a shower a clean shirt, and a drink. It was then that I discovered we were out of water. The gauge, like the gas gauge registered half full, but that was a little joke on me. I walked around to the rear of the bus where the water tank was located, opened the cap, and looked in. There was little to see, so I announced to my crew that we had an empty water tank, a full river, and lots of pans. I gave each girl a pan, lined them up the riverbank between the water and the bus, and urged them to dish the Walker River into the tank. It was slow going but very invigorating for them, I thought. It would either teach them self-sufficiency or give them an appreciation of the ranch. An hour later I got a trickle from the shower, so I urged them on again, promising enough water for everybody. Meanwhile, I decided our camp would also make a good dumping station, so I attached a large snakelike plastic hose to an outlet beneath the bus and pulled the plug.

A rush of water quickly blew the hose off the outlet and poured out around us, soaking the campfire and driving my bucket brigade to higher ground. Puddles of bluish water surrounded the bus, soaking slowly into the ground.

"This isn't a dumping station," Freddie cried from a rock in the middle of the river.

"It is now," I told her. "I'll add it to the list."

"Now we can't have a fire, Daddy."

"You're polluting the river," Susie helpfully complained.

"Back to the pans," I told them. "It holds about fifty gallons."

They worked pouring water into the tank until dark. The gauge showed it to be half full, and I decided to skip my shower and use the water for a highball instead. We prepared a cold supper out of our leftover lunch, went through the incredible bed-making performance again, this time losing Hari under the piles of blankets, and finally settled down on our small shelves for the night. The roar of the river behind us and the passing trucks on the highway in front of us drowned out the trickle of melting ice cubes inside the tilted refrigerator. Somebody laughed.

"I bet nobody ever filled a water tank that way before."

"Could we spend tomorrow night in a hotel?"

"Yes, then we could all take a shower."

"Good night!" I called from the top shelf.

In the morning, after a breakfast of warm orange juice, cold toast and Walker River coffee, I headed the bus for Lake Tahoe and civilization. I dreamed of beds and bathrooms and plumbing I didn't have to worry about, and, as I pushed up and over the

115

mountains to the lake, in Mark Twain's words, "I thought it must surely be the fairest picture the whole earth affords." We rolled into the hotel parking lot at noon and, leaving Hari wagging in the front seat, we moved into luxurious rooms. Cowardly camper that I am, I surrendered to room service and lay flat on my back for the first time since leaving Los Angeles. And there we lingered for two days, while I suffered and recovered from a delayed attack of motor-home nerves, and the showers ran, and we could wash both hands at once.

I missed the ranch and Dee and Corporal Salt, and after two nights of rest was eager to turn the bus south toward them. Of course, four hundred miles lay between me and those precious seven acres, with another night of camping along the way, but it would be easy now. There must be a place somewhere along the California coast where we could park long enough to rest and prepare for the long-awaited greeting from my herd. I could see them now, raising their heads from the tall grass, pleased that I had survived the long, insane journey. We left the lake in high spirits, heading for Sacramento, Simon and Garfunkel and Hari again filling the air with song.

I had devised a skillful bit of navigation which, according to my plan, would take us south and east from Sacramento over a series of obscure routes to the coast. There we would drive through the Big Sur country to San Luis Obispo, and from there to the ranch, where I hoped to blow up the bus and forget it. While Freddie turned the map around hunting for my route numbers I drove through the outskirts of Sacramento and on to the flat red earth of Central California. We were out of food, so we paused at a hamburger stand slightly smaller than the bus for lunch, then on again heading west, over-confident.

It took us four hours on my short cuts to make the two-hour trip from Sacramento to Oakland and San Francisco, the two cities I wanted desperately to avoid. By an intricate system of wrong turns we found ourselves on the Bay Bridge in rush-hour traffic, stopped like a white elephant in a pack of jackals, three hours from the Monterey Peninsula and those pine trees. We crawled along

116

with the commuters through the cocktail hour, stopping only long enough to buy eleven dollars' worth of gas below San Francisco, where the attendant asked me how to get rid of termites.

I gave him a withering look.

"Thought you was one of those exterminator outfits," he said.

"I'm a rancher," I told him. "Got a big spread south of here."

"How many head you run?"

Staring straight into his shifty little eyes I said, "Six."

"Wow," he exclaimed, shaking his head in wonder and admiration for a man who owned six hundred, or, perhaps six thousand cattle. Let him wonder! Let him admire!

It was dark when we drove through Monterey, heading for Carmel and our campsite, but I found the pines, the beach, the sea at the foot of the main street and collapsed over the steering wheel.

"Change for dinner," I called. "This is the end of the line."

"There's a police car behind us," Nicole announced.

A flashlight shone in my face, a badge glittering outside my window, and we were ordered to move. No Campers. No Parking. No Rest. I drove back through Carmel and in desperation pulled into a large parking area behind the I. Magnin store to reconnoiter. The shoppers were gone, the lot was deserted except for a fleet of delivery trucks parked in a dark corner, and I saw my big chance. I drove the bus into the midst of the trucks and quickly turned off the lights.

"Dress in the dark," I called to my passengers. "We'll find a place to eat on foot."

We did, and ate cold spaghetti in a small Italian coffee shop trying its best to close for the night. Then back to the bus and the bed-making, this time without a light. We had found a campsite, and there in picturesque old Carmel, within a mere mile of pines and the cries of gulls, we nestled among the trucks like thieves.

"I haven't paid my I. Magnin bill," Freddie called softly.

"We'll be gone before the store opens," I reassured her.

Dawn that Saturday in Carmel was so cold with fog so thick that the trucks around us were veiled, dark shapes. We felt safe enough to turn on the lights and sipped cups of tea and coffee while we tucked away the mountain of sheets and blankets for the last time. Then, cautiously, I slipped out from behind the trucks and across the empty parking lot into the street. By the time the rest of the town was up we were moving slowly through the fog to the coast road, Big Sur, and the ranch. And, as if we were following the script of a Western, leaving the charred remains of our homestead behind to begin a new life after the last of the Sioux has ridden over the hill, we drove into bright sunshine ten miles outside Carmel. The winding empty road wound away in front of me as the bus edged along those famous precipices and my family aahed at the view. We were heading home. Simon and Garfunkel and Hari and I sang.

At the stroke of three I drove down Solvang's Mission Drive and on out of town to Refugio Road. Past the familiar landmarks, the walnut groves, the rolling fields of alfalfa we drove to the dirt road and turned. Windows were open, music on full blast, and Jeremy and Nicole leaned from the bus, shouting, "Hi, Corporal, Hi, Sergeant, Hi, Lieutenant!"

My herd looked up from a clover patch near the road as the great white hulk moved toward them, ablast with sound. Then with a frightened bellow they ran for the opposite fence their tails trailing straight out behind them like pirates' pennants.

Through the fence they went as if it had been strung by a minor spider, and into a neighboring field.

"They've forgotten us," Jeremy cried.

"They just don't recognize us in this bus," Nicole corrected her.

"What would you do if you saw a house covered with spiders and blasting rock 'n roll music chasing you?" Susie asked.

"Stampede," I shouted.

"Exactly," she said.

10

"What, is the jay more precious than the lark,
because his feathers are more beautiful?"
- WILLIAM SHAKESPEARE

The stampede fizzled out just beyond the fence. Like a defensive line that suddenly discovers the quarterback went the other way, my three steers stopped and looked back at the shredded fence and were sorry. Then, trying to pretend they had not made fools of themselves, they self-consciously bent their heads to the ground and nibbled the parched grass in the neighboring field. Dee, who had watched the stampede from a safe distance, returned to her grazing. I drove on into the ranch driveway, issuing a volley of instructions.

While my family moved out of the motor home and into the house, I put on my boots and headed for the field. I was ashamed to call on Nielson Downs again, determined to round up my own herd if it took a week. I found the hole, which, as before, seemed much to small to push a steer through, even if he scrunched up, and Corporal, Sergeant, and Lieutenant wandered over on their side of the barbed wire to watch me. The green grass on my side and the brown weeds on theirs should have made them try, but they obviously were not going to, so with pliers and hammer I made the hole larger. I even tied the strands of wire together with baling wire until the hole was as large as they were. They looked interested, but that was all. I crawled back and forth under the wire to show them how easy it was and even pushed Corporal toward the hole, but they would not believe me. I tried crying "Ho" again and even "Please!" but they just blinked and backed off.

Then I hit on an idea. I walked back to the stable and filled a pail with Dee's grain, a sticky mixture of oats and molasses with an enticing candy smell. I carried the pail to the fence hole, set it a few feet inside the fence where my steers could not lean in to reach it, and watched them sniff the sweetened breeze from my side. I backed off. They put their heads into the hole and licked their lips with large purple tongues. I backed off farther. Then I turned my back and pretended to be looking for a four-leaf clover, peeking occasionally. They tested the hole, and at last Corporal got down on his knees and edged into the field to the bucket of grain. Sergeant and Lieutenant could stand it no longer. They followed, and once again my herd was in my field, stuffing their noses into the pail. I rushed back to let down the barbed wire, fastening it and stapling it as quickly as I could.

I sauntered back to the house, hoping someone would ask me how I intended to rescue the herd, but they were all unpacking and mixing cool drinks, as if a stampede was no more important than an extra earwig in the sink.

"Got 'em in," I announced, breathing hard to impress someone.

"That's nice," Nicole called from the kitchen.

Just wait, I thought. I'll tell this story at the Pancake House. I'll impress those pastry-eating cowboys. Rounded up a spooked herd, I did, with no help from anybody. It was good to know I hadn't lost my touch.

"Take my boots off," I called to everybody.

A week later the motor home was a fading memory. My knuckles, bruised by the emergency-brake handle, my back, bowed by nights curled on my sleeping shelf, were healing, and cramping was no longer mentioned. The calves, pleased to see the blue truck arriving again, resumed their midsummer siestas, and the days were cool and hot and cool. Only Dee refused to adjust to the lazy life of a single girl. While the ghost of Pancho lingered beyond the fence line she fussed, submitting to shampoos and combing but never to Jeremy's attempts to ride her. When she saw the bridle, she clenched her teeth, raised her chin, and blew through her nostrils. When the saddle appeared, she prepared herself so that just as I heaved it up over her back she sidestepped, and watched as I wound up on my knees, the saddle in the dirt. Once mounted, Jeremy could do little more than walk her in ever-diminishing circles until Dee won and was allowed to race to the end of the field to take up her stand at the fence.

Riding lessons were the only solution, and my fence builder, Magnus Jepson, suggested a teacher he knew. Another phone call and all was arranged for Jeremy's first riding lesson the following Saturday. Nancy Schley strode into the yard looking at first like a female version of Willie Shoemaker, tiny, brisk, and very professional. In dusty boots, tight dungarees, and open Western shirt, dark hair brushed straight back and efficiently bunned out of the way, she took charge of my daughter and her horse in the first few minutes of our acquaintance, and at the end of the first hour had all of us obeying her instructions to the letter. Dee, overwhelmed by so many commands, went wherever she was ordered to go, while Jeremy became the first member of my family ever to gain the upper hand with an animal.

While the Valley bloomed in the final celebration of August, then began its slow submission to the parched days of September and October when southern California wilts like a week-old rose. Jeremy and Dee and Nancy Schley extended their lessons. At first I watched them move down the dirt road, now walking, now trotting, now stopping to test their new relationship. Then one weekend Nancy arrived in a pickup towing a horse trailer, and off she and Jeremy and Dee went to ride on more distant trails. Now the lessons became half-day excursions, with Dee and Jeremy arriving back at the ranch hot and happy, each apparently satisfied that the age-old relationship between horse and rider had been reestablished.

We arrived at the ranch for the long Thanksgiving weekend after dark and went searching for animals with a flashlight. As usual, the calves were first to recognize the sounds of the truck, Fernando's proprietary bark, and the opening of the stable door. Late November left little to eat in the frostbitten pasture, and our arrival meant hay in three small piles around the water trough. The herd was in place and waiting. Then, out of the black noses behind the steers two larger shapes moved toward the corral.

"It's Prince," Jeremy cried.

"Who?" I asked, watching two shapes approach.

"He's a horse we know. Mrs. Schley said she wanted to hide him here for awhile. I forgot to tell you."

"Hide him from what?"

"His owners," Jeremy explained.

Here I was, the owner of a registered brand, accepted by the entire Valley as the new, legitimate owner of the Small ranch, a horse rustler. Where would it all end? I opened the corral gate, and as Dee passed me on her way to her hay pile, a large Palomino followed docilely behind her. It was too dark to see more of the horse than the part revealed by the flashlight, so I put out a second pile of hay, closed the gate, and retreated. I was relieved when the light was off and the corral, dark and silent again, I walked quickly to the house, mixed a drink, and sank low in my chair.

"If Mrs. Schley wants to steal horses, I'll thank her to hide them somewhere else," I told Jeremy.

"Oh, Daddy, she's just leaving him here for a while."

"Suppose they find him here," I said, the thundering hooves of the sheriff's posse drumming in my ears.

"Nobody'll blame you. Anyway, now Dee has company, except she doesn't like him."

"Why?" I asked her.

"Oh, nobody likes Prince very much."

"He must be quite a horse."

122

"You can meet him tomorrow," Jeremy said.

All it takes on a late fall morning is the first pink glow from the rising sun to move the steers slowly down the field toward breakfast. At the fence opposite my bedroom window they pause to watch and listen, offering a low hint now and then that morning has arrived. The closing of the bedroom window, the opening of a door to allow Fernando to move toward them across the frost-tipped grass, confirm for them my awareness, and the hints swell to demands. Off they move to the corral, while I move to meet them, Hay is loosened and carried to them in generous forkfuls while they jostle each other for position, white breath rising into the brightening day.

Just as I completed my breakfast service to the steers that morning Dee appeared, walking her roundabout way to the corral, as if she hated to admit that she liked the menu. And at a respectful distance behind her came Prince, walking stiffly like a furry rocking horse. I opened the gate as Dee arrived and invited her in to dine without interference from the steers. She moved into the corral, Prince behind her, where I had prepared two separate piles of hay, and at last I had an opportunity to examine this strange new addition to the ranch.

The first thing I noticed about my rustled horse was that he wore a winter coat of thick, golden-orange hair which stuck out from his body, blurring his profile. He was the first completely shaggy horse I had ever seen. The long hair grew down his legs and over the tops of his hooves, so that as he stood with his legs too close together he looked like a man wearing loose pajama bottoms. His back, beneath the bristling hair, was concave except for a prominent lump at just about the place where a rider would sit, and his neck rose out of this great depression like a roll-up shag rug. Prince's face was even stranger. His long nose rose into a high ridge which seemed to go on forever before it reached his eyes, giving him the appearance of a huge stuffed camel, while his eyes were those of an animal that never gets enough sleep. In fact, each time he blinked it took longer for the lids to go up again, until at last he simply sighed and let them droop and took a short nap while I sighted along his nose. When he lowered his head to eat, he chewed so slowly that I decided he must have a lot on his mind.

I have met men like Prince, men who always appear to have gotten out of bed too soon, who say little and say it slowly, who scratch themselves and stare blankly at the world around them. Their friends think of them as deep thinkers. Other people wonder why they bothered to get up at all. This great, contemplative horse gave no indication of his feelings, accepting me and Dee and the mound of hay with the same dreamlike stoicism he might have shown toward an abusing child, a badgering horse, or no hay at all. I wondered if he had ever kicked up those funny, furry heels or cried out with joy. I wondered too who had named him Prince. Was his name someone's idea of a cruel joke, or had a spindly golden foal once seemed princely? I preferred to think he had once deserved his royal name as I watched him slowly chewing his first breakfast with us. As I gently wiped the tearing matter from the corners of his great, sleepy eyes I hoped he would never be found. It was no longer true that nobody liked Prince.

The relationship between Dee and Prince had already been settled by the time I met Prince. In the corral that first morning he followed wherever Dee lead, from post to post, at a distance of about two feet, head slightly lowered, eyes straight ahead, like a man following his wife through a lingerie department. Dee, on the other hand, ignored her camel-faced suitor, swishing her tail in his face, laying her ears back whenever this big orange horse moved around to the front to see how he was making out. Across a barbed-wire fence Pancho had looked good. Now, apparently, Prince looked terrible, and Dee had no use for him. I was beginning to understand the life Prince must have led, ignored by mares, despised by humans, crowded by cattle. No wonder he kept his eyes closed most of the time.

We kept both horses in the corral all morning, serving separate hay piles and alternating them between the expensive pride of the two-horse owner and the furtive guilt of the one-horse stealer. Nothing happened. Prince chewed and slept, while Dee sulked in a corner and compared him unfavorably with Pancho. Jeremy polished Dee and Prince looked on, but she moved over to comb his coat at last, and Prince emerged from this treatment looking like a hippie horse. At noon Nancy Schley, her husband, and their truck and trailer rolled into the driveway for Jeremy's lesson, and I hurried out to discuss Prince.

"I understand I am harboring a stolen horse," I complained. "And just when I promised Sacramento to help stamp out rustling."

The Schleys laughed. "Not really stolen," Nancy said. "We sort of borrowed Prince. His owners want to sell him, but they overpaid and nobody will buy him. So until they can get him into the stockyards he doesn't get much to eat. It's really sad."

"Stockyards?"

"You know, for dog food. That's the only way they can sell him."

I looked over to see Prince chew once and fall into a deep sleep, the sun on his furry back, one rear hoof resting lightly against the other. With his caved in back, his lump, and two sets of seemingly unrelated legs in baggy fur pants he looked at that moment like two men dressed in a horse suit with the rear man taking a lunch break.

"Do you think they'll find him?" I asked.

"Oh, no. Not for a week or two. Then we'll move him someplace else."

As Jeremy led Dee from the stable to the trailer, I assured the Schleys that Prince had a home on the ranch for as long as he wanted it. I remembered the auction at the stockyards and the old horses being led through. How could anyone sell Prince for ten cents a pound? I went over to the rail and fed him a sugar lump and scratched his nose.

"Don't worry," I whispered to him. He opened one eye and closed it again. He wasn't worried.

When Jeremy, Dee and the Schleys were disappearing down our road in a dust cloud through which Dee's bay bottom was barely visible, Prince woke up. A shrill neigh shattered the crisp November air, and when I turned to the corral, Prince was trotting busily back and forth in a nervous state so acute that his eyes were open, his head up, and his tail alert behind him. Dee was gone! And just when old Prince had decided that his sleepy adoration, if not welcome, was at least tolerated. I returned to put out more hay, but Prince ran through it without noticing. I patted his long arching nose, but he looked down at me as if I were the latest in the line of treacherous humans. I opened the gate and let him out to allow more room for his thousand-pound frustration. There, outside the corral, I witnessed one of the great moments in the old horse's life. He ran a few yards. Then, with a giant effort, he actually kicked up his heels. I wouldn't describe it as bucking. It was more like the effort a man might make in attempting to jump over a rock with both feet securely tied together at the ankles. Prince's two stiff hind legs came up in the air close together, then out behind him, as if he were imitating a horse. It was an exciting moment.

Then he trotted up the pasture, neighing long, high cries of longing, unable to find Dee, unable to believe he had been deserted. I retreated to the ranch for a nap, but there was no sleep for either Prince or me that afternoon. He paced back and forth, and his frantic cries could be heard going and coming past my window.

Dee returned in the late afternoon twilight, and both horses settled again in the corral, while the steers munched beyond the fence.

"What do you think they'd take for Prince?" I asked Jeremy.

"Mrs. Schley thinks they could get at least a hundred dollars at the stockyards. But, Daddy, maybe they won't find him." She sat beside me at our table, frowning as deeply as a young girl with a smooth forehead can frown. "We don't feed Fernando horse meat, do we?"

"We feed him beef," I reminded her.

Jeremy looked up. "Oh, Daddy," she said, and sighed.

On that Saturday it rained. A rancher's responsibilities to his livestock continue even in the rain, which settles in silvery drops on the backs of the steers and stains the horses' coats. But rain does not settle in silvery drops on what little hair I have, so I drove to Solvang to buy my first cowboy hat. I wanted one stained by dust and sweat of cattle drives like Eric Fleming's, but of course they had no stained ones. I tried on several large Western hats, but I seemed to look more like Dan Blocker in *Bonanza* than Eric Fleming in *Rawhide*, until I decided to buy one too small for me. Immediately, it gave me a jaunty look like Clint Eastwood, unless I leaned over too far, when it fell on the floor. I bought it and wore it out of the store, hoping the rain would weather it quickly before anyone saw me.

It is the law of the West that a cowboy dresses from top to bottom and undresses from bottom to top. Everybody knows that, and the cowboy's favorite hat remains on his head when everything else he wears is strewn around the campfire. Not wanting to break any more laws, I tried it, with unfortunate results. After I'd fed the horses and cattle that evening I lay back on the bed holding my hat on and ordered Jeremy to remove my boots. Difficult as that was to accomplish, removing socks and pants was even more difficult. Every time I bent down my hat fell off. I don't know how those early riders of the purple sage accomplished it, unless their hats were glued on.

As for dressing in the morning, it was rather unsettling to stand before the bathroom mirror brushing my teeth with my Western hat tilted at a carefree angle, and the moment I stepped into my shorts the damned hat hit the floor again. I want to take my proper place in the West, respecting its customs, perhaps even becoming a legend, but a cowboy whose hat falls off every time he leans over and who has to rely on a young girl to pull his boots off can hardly expect to strike fear in the hearts of cattle thieves and claim-jumpers.

Prince stayed on. He was there shadowing Dee the following weekend, and I must admit I was pleased. Because Jeremy had a friend along, Prince was hauled off in the trailer with Dee to the riding lesson. The little girl who rode him complained that he would only walk behind Dee and that his lump was uncomfortable to sit on, but Prince enjoyed it. His leaving was simply not mentioned, and whenever I inquired, Jeremy shrugged and accepted the horse's uncertain future.

At lunch in Hollywood a couple of weeks after Prince's arrival I sat listening to the pet woes of two of my friends. These men, occupied with professions and golf and teenage children and house repairs, as are most of the men I know, had each devoted a recent day to his sick cat. Each had rushed a frightened feline to a vet, stayed with the cat through minor surgery and carried it home again, where the cats were nursed and babied back to health. They sat at lunch with me comparing their experiences with cat catastrophes, while I nodded and sympathized. I had not known until then that an ailing cat could cause either of them to drop everything else. But my friends, Phil Zeller and Arthur Volando, supersalesmen in the music business, were pushovers when their cats were ailing. So I told them about Prince and his destiny.

"You mean he's going to be sold for dog food?" Phil asked, horrified.

"Not if I can help it," I told him.

"How much do they want?" Artie asked.

I told them my guess was about a hundred dollars.

Zeller reached for his wallet. "I'll buy a quarter of Prince," he said, handing me twenty-five dollars.

"And I'll buy another quarter," Artie said, writing out a check.

"You just bought half a horse," I announced "You can have either half, but I'd suggest the rear. The front is asleep."

Half of Prince had been rescued by a couple of cat lovers who had never met him. I would rescue the other half. I left my two friends after lunch, but as I watched them walk up that Hollywood street, as so often happens, the world seemed a better place than it was. Compassion for a sick cat or an old, doomed horse, or for that matter, any living thing is nice to find on a busy day. My two friends had demonstrated what seems to me to be so badly needed: the realization that in nature all things are unique and therefore precious.

On a Saturday morning early in February I was sitting on my stool at the Pancake House sipping coffee with Jim Farmer and his little group of rancheros. My hat, suitably shabby now from falling off so often, was hanging beside theirs, my boots were muddy after two months of excessive rain, and my dungarees were covered with hayseeds. I looked even ranchier than my companions and was well informed on rainfall, scarcity of hay, and the stock market, our topics for the morning.

"How's the mare?" Mrs. Santangelo asked as she refilled my cup.

"Fine," I told her. "At the moment she's between love affairs, though, and Jeremy has all she can do to handle her."

"Why don't you breed her?" she suggested. "She's foaled before, you know."

"I know where you can get her bred," Jim Farmer chimed in. "There's an old white quarter horse over at Lee Burr's who's the best stud around. Come on to the office and we'll call him."

It was a wild suggestion, it seemed to me, and an involved way of settling a horse's problems, but I was learning that ranching impels a man ever onward and that each problem is resolved only by a more complicated and usually expensive solution. It is like winning an elephant in a quiz show and ending up having to move to Africa. I followed Jim to his office to call Lee Burr, who turned out to be the foreman of a large Thoroughbred ranch in the Valley.

"Say, Lee, you still got that white quarter horse stud?"

I shifted in my chair, tempted to shout "No! Wait!"

"Well, a friend of mine's got a little mare he wants to breed. How about taking her on?"

There was a small pause while Burr, I suppose, consulted his horse.

"Yeah, he bought the Small ranch. I'll send him over."

Farmer hung up the phone. "Sure, he'll take her just for boarding fees. Won't cost you anything in stud fees."

I almost said, "Gee, a free foal," but I didn't.

I got directions to the Curragh Stock Farm and headed home to tell Jeremy she was going to be a grandmother. The whole arrangement seemed presumptuous to me, but then a horse breeder is a man, not a horse, just as a mink farmer is not a mink or

129

even a farmer, so I suppose I was within my rights, even if I was out of my mind. If love would leave Jeremy's horse calm and happy, what were a few minor expenses? Anyway, as a I remembered from my horse books, nothing would happen for eleven months. I turned into the driveway feeling like the father of the bride.

11

"However one may view it, man is in course of transforming the rest of the animals or killing them with his shadow."
- PIERRE TEILHARD DE CHARDIN

Southeast across the Valley floor the ranches are large and businesslike. Here acres are measured in hundreds, cattle are small, brown flecks against the rolling hills, and the only buildings in sight are ranch houses flanked by hay barns, roofs supported by corner posts, like houses without walls. In late February this part of the Valley is a vast green threshold leading to the mountains, with little to interrupt its flat, grassy surface. Windmills, usually on their last three legs from buffeting winds, still stand here and there, and in the distance plumes of smoke rise where ranchers take advantage of the windless mornings to burn accumulated brush. But even these so-called controlled burns are disappearing from the morning landscape, for the Valley, like the world, is worried now about its atmosphere. For the first time since man discovered the uses of fire there is concern not for what may burn, but for what may not, and the legal fire may soon become illegal.

Jeremy and I drove across this open country in the truck, headed for the Curragh Stock Farm and Dee's future mate. Fernando rode in the truck bed, standing to sniff the interesting wind as it blew along at an intersection of two roads and turned into a winding path leading us past more horses than we had ever seen in one place before.

A stock farm is the apparently successful proof that the Darwinian laws of natural selection have been replaced by the laws of human selection. Wherever man has found animals useful to him and willing to breed under his scrutiny he has taken over the responsibility for improving the species. In doing so he has emphasized the parts of each animal most profitable to himself, reducing or eliminating the rest, until the Angus steer, for example, has become a creature with a huge body and practically no legs. If man is successful, future generations of Angus cattle will balance their thousand-pound bodies on casterlike hooves. They will not run to a pile of hay or step over a badger hole or kick up their heels on a spring morning. Instead, they will wobble to the feed trough and grow fatter. And for the Angus, according to the laws of human selection, that is enough.

At the ranch we entered that morning the business was raising Thoroughbreds. Hundreds of acres of lush, green pasture had been fenced into aristocratic paddocks, each containing six or eight gleaming young horses. On a hillside sleek mares stood while week-old foals nuzzled beneath their sleek bellies for milk, and in an adjacent pasture thick-waisted mares waited for foaling time. A restless stallion paced his paddock, head high, nostrils wide as the breeze carried all this marish excitement to him. Here the horses were bred according to their family trees, and their offspring were sold after a year for as much as new Cadillacs. There was no doubt that we were entering into the highest horse society.

"I wonder how Dee will look among all those snobbish Thoroughbreds," I said to Jeremy as we bounded along the dirt road.

"I think she's prettier than they are," my daughter answered. "She has an Arabian head, and after all, that's where Thoroughbreds come from."

"You're right, Stub. She's just as good as they are."

At the end of the winding path through Thoroughbred country we came to a gravel parking lot, a sweep of immaculate, shaded lawn, and a white ranch house, headquarters for the foreman. Next to the house were two large trailers, permanently parked, the modern version of the Western bunkhouse. An old man was pushing a wheelbarrow along the driveway picking up dung with a shovel, while a younger man on a tractor towed fresh hay to the brood mares beyond the fence. On a knoll overlooking the ranch was the heart of the stock farm, a fortresslike building freshly painted, where the important residents of the ranch lived. This was the stable, and Jeremy and I headed for it, leaving Fernando to bark at expensive horses. Inside, we discovered a square of stalls, each facing a grassy courtyard, and at our approach a dozen elegant noses appeared in the stall openings. These, we later learned, were yearlings, last year's foals, being readied for annual sale. They had never seen a track or felt a jockey, but their parents and grandparents were racers, and that was to be their destiny. After giving us a superior glance, they turned away.

In one of the stalls was a gathering of horses and humans. A man who I guessed was Lee Burr held a foal in a sweeping embrace, while another man in a long white smock filled a syringe with liquid. A large bay mare stood by watching her new son get his first shot. Jeremy and I watched too from outside the stall, intrigued by our first close look at a newborn horse. When the shot had been given, I introduced myself.

"You're the fella with the mare," he observed shrewdly. "Want to see Joe?"

"Joe who?"

"Joe the Teaser," Burr said, making everything clear.

We followed him along the shaded stable path and back

133

down the hill to a row of boarded corrals. At one he stopped and leaned across the fence motioning us to lean beside him. There, posing in a corner as if he were modeling for a new monument, was a white quarter horse with muscles flexed like an equine Charles Atlas.

"That's old Joe," Burr said.

"How old is he?" Jeremy asked.

"I figure about thirty, honey," Burr told her.

"Can he still, er, ah...?" I asked.

"Old Joe? Don't worry about him. He's the best teaser in the Valley."

Whatever Joe was, I believed it. As we watched, he shifted his weight to another hoof, his muscles bulging. Maybe he thought we were a new lot of romantic mares. At any rate, he whiffled softly and turned away, ignoring us and loving every minute of it.

I decided to continue my policy of waiting for answers rather than asking foolish questions. Lee Burr was not a man to volunteer information he thought everybody ought to know, so our relationship got off to a slow start. As we turned from the corral to walk back to my truck, I had no idea what Joe or Burr had in mind. Jeremy also remained silent, figuring her father would explain everything later. Her confidence in me, misplaced though it might be, was nevertheless heartening.

"You bought the Small place?" Burr finally asked. I thought he never would.

I nodded.

"You don't have a trailer?"

I shook my head.

"Well, we get over that way pretty often. I'll pick up the mare next time I'm by there. We'll keep her here till she comes in heat."

"When will that be, Mr. Burr?" I asked, hating myself.

"Should be every fifteen days or so. Joe will know."

"I bet he will," I laughed hollowly. That musclebound old egomaniac is going to be the father of Dee's foal, I remembered. But I didn't like his methods, so I decided to break my rule before committing her. "What is a teaser?" I asked.

Burr looked at me patiently out of appraising brown eyes, shining like berries in a stand of cactus. "A teaser teases the mares," he explained.

I nodded, grateful to have that problem cleared up. "Well, you pick her up when you can."

Jeremy and I drove back down the path in silence. When we were once again on the road home, she asked, "Why does he tease the mares?"

"I guess he's like some people," I told her. "He enjoys it."

"Come on, Daddy, why does he tease the mares?"

"I think I know, Stub, but we'll ask Jim Farmer."

We drove back to the ranch to meet Dee and Prince. It was good to wipe the tears from Prince's eye again. I had had enough of conceited superhorses for one day.

My investigation of Joe the Teaser began with a call to Jim Farmer that evening. My excuse was to thank him for arranging the whole thing, but I wasted no time getting to Joe. "Just what does that horse do?" I asked. "He looks so self satisfied."

"He's a teaser," Farmer said, using that word again. "They use him to stir up the mares. He'll walk up to one mare after another, and if she's ready she shows it when she sees Joe. Then they hustle him out and bring in the Thoroughbred stallion for breeding."

"You mean all he does is get them all riled up and then walks off while another horse is having all the fun? Why does he look so smug?"

"Don't worry about Joe. I've got one horse he sired, and half the people up here take their mares to Joe. He isn't frustrated."

And so it was. Nielson Downs told me Joe had fathered a foal of his. At Mattei's Tavern, when the news was out about Dee, there were knowing nods all over the bar. "Joe the Teaser, eh. He's some horse!" At the Pancake House a week later the stool-riding cowboys all congratulated me on Joe the Teaser. "If he was a man, he'd be ninety," Ed McCarty exclaimed, shaking his head in wonder. Yes, Joe the Teaser was some horse. No wonder he was always posing. And what a career! What better life for man or animal than to combine vocation with avocation? Every day Joe displayed his alabaster physique, his marble muscles to a bunch of panting girls, nonchalantly walking away, smiling a superior smile, then moonlighting all over the Valley in his free time. He was like a wine taster who goes home each night to a full bottle.

In the final days of February Dee was hauled off to her rendezvous with Joe. We arrived for our weekend to find Prince, his cheeks damp, standing alone at the end of the field, and he was pleased to know that part, at least, of the small new world he discovered was still intact. Jeremy brushed him, I fed him, and the steers envied him, all of which, for Prince, was consoling. But we were anxious to get to Dee, so we canceled a trip to the dump to head for the Stock Farm. We found Lee Burr, this time painting the injured leg of a prized Thoroughbred with medicine, and, when this was done, he looked up and seemed to recognize me. (He had a way of looking at me that seemed to say, "I know you from somewhere, but it doesn't much matter where.")

"You're mare's down behind the house," he said. "She must have just gone out of heat when we picked her up."

"Maybe she doesn't like Joe."

Burr looked at me as if I had lost my marbles. "She'll like him when she's ready." He scratched his chin. "Come on. Let's walk Joe down to her. He hasn't seen her today."

Burr put a lead rope on the mighty Joe, and the four of us walked down the path to a corral behind the ranch house. There in a muddy enclosure was Dee, nibbling hay and looking sensationally bored. Jeremy pulled up a handful of long grass growing beside the fence and called to Dee, who turned and walked slowly toward us. When she arrived at the fence, Burr led Joe up to her. The two horses, nose to nose, shared the grass in Jeremy's hand, about as interested in each other as a couple of subway riders.

"Not yet," Lee Burr said and turned back down the path, followed by the Teaser. "Maybe by the next time you come up."

Jeremy and I stayed to visit Dee for a while, then returned to the ranch. We could lead our horse to love, but... I received a bill

136

from the stock farm for two weeks' board at three dollars a day, but... And then, just after mid-March, we climbed to the stable to find Lee Burr and received the news. Joe had finally met Dee on the right day, and all went well. Burr showed me a chart with days marked off by a slanting, penciled line to March 12, where there was a large "X." What a day that must have been!

"We better keep her another two weeks," he said, "just to be sure."

I agreed. How could I disagree? We visited Dee, who was muddy and as bored as ever, but we treated her with new respect. She was now an expectant mother and one more conquest for Joe the Teaser, who was probably back in his corral posing for another monument, the whole incident forgotten in the sexual welter that made up his days. We drove home that day fulfilled. We had done it! A free foal for only $125 worth of boarding bills from the famous Joe the Teaser.

"Maybe you'll get a buckskin," Jim Farmer said when I told him.

"You may get a Palomino," Betty McClellan said when I was toasted that night at Mattei's.

"I just want a foal," Jeremy said softly.

It had been an exciting adventure.

It was April again, our second April as ranchers, and an easy, bountiful time on the Small ranch. The steers were busy gaining their pound and a half a day in tall grass still growing without help from me and my pipes. Dee was back and, as predicted, she had a new personality. Jeremy rode her across the fields and along the road without difficulty. Dee accepted commands and compliments calmly. The long riding lessons resumed, while Magnus Jepson and I waged our war on the weeds and strung more barbed wire along the fences to keep the steers from pushing out the rails. Prince, happy to be following in Dee's wake, even if it meant inheriting a few of her flies, was part of our family. It was a peaceful month when all the living things around us bloomed without aid from me. Then came a call from Nancy Schley.

137

"Prince's owners know where he is," she told me. "They want him back."

"For dog food?"

"A hundred dollars' worth."

This was no time of year to be canned, not with warm sunshine and burr clover and golden sunsets. "I'll give you a check," I told her.

Nancy laughed. "I knew you'd say that. If you hadn't, I was going to hide him again."

"Jeremy will have the check when you pick her up today."

I told my daughter, who immediately went to the corral to pat the lumpy old horse. Prince was ours, shared, of course, by my two Hollywood friends. I followed Jeremy to the corral to congratulate my half.

According to instructions from Lee Burr we called in a vet on the 1st of May to confirm Dee's pregnancy. He arrived in his covered pickup and followed me out to the corral, carrying his medical bag. There he fastened a twisted chain to the tip of Dee's nose, showed me how to hold it, and ran around behind the horse. I watched him pull on a long rubber glove and prepare to attack Dee from the rear. I stood still, feeling my toes being flattened, not daring to move during this precarious probe.

My eyes were filling with tears as the vet withdrew his arm. "Forty-five days in foal," he called. "Yessir, a thrifty little mare. A thrifty little mare."

I couldn't answer him. He saw me then and came around the horse to pat me on the back sympathetically.

"I guess you've been worried," he said.

"It is good to know everything's all right," I replied, wiping my cheeks. He walked out of the corral with me, his arm around my shoulder.

The hiatus of April vanished with the warming sun. Once again it was time to move the pipes into the field for another summer of irrigation. The three new calves settled down, following

138

their elders around like small helpers, while I stared and stalled over Corporal, Sergeant, and Lieutenant, knowing I should sell them, determined not to. Our precious pasture was covered with animals, all nibbling at once, and Nielson Downs called every week or two to tell me that beef prices were at an all-time high. Then, to compound our problem, I discovered Jeremy out in the field with her arm around one of the new calves. We had been kissed and followed and nuzzled by the old steers, but this was the first time one of the calves had submitted to being embraced.

"Look, Daddy. I've named him Pigget. So far he's the tamest."

"How about the other two?"

"I'm still thinking," she said and tried to frown.

"I think I'll name one Ham and the other Burger," I told her, "just to get some kind of perspective around here."

It was then that the phone rang. I ran to the house to hear my friend Lou calling from Phoenix. He was full of questions.

"Did you get an offer on the ranch?"

"No," I told him.

"Did you sell any cows?"

"No," I said, "but I just bought three more and another horse."

"Did you sell anything?"

"Not a thing."

"I better come up next weekend. We'll have a little talk."

City dwellers will never understand the pressures of ranching. I agreed to meet him in Los Angeles and drive him to the ranch. I'll talk, I told myself, but I won't sell a friend. My steers must have overheard me. They bellowed softly and moved to meet me for dinner.

Lou rode to the ranch with me on a bright Saturday morning, saving his suggestions for our arrival. Once there, however, he was all business, rubbing his hands together in anticipation of something or other. To please him Magnus Jepson and I recently planted two small peach trees, and he could hardly wait to see them. Lou likes fruit. He loves deductible fruit, so we walked briskly to a patch of dirt he was already calling "the orchard" where his face fell perceptibly when he found that my peach trees were two small twigs valiantly attempting to stay alive.

"How soon will there be peaches?" he asked, looking down at one of the twigs, which bore two leaves fluttering at the very top.

"Maybe two years," I told him.

"Well, let's look at the cows."

We walked to the corral where the herd was waiting for what was now brunch. While I carried hay to them, Lou leaned over the water trough, staring at the eager faces of Corporal, Sergeant, and Lieutenant. Three new calves, jostled out of position, watched from a distance. As I carried the first pitchfork of hay to the steers, I saw Lou put out a hand to scratch Corporal's lumpy head.

"How much can you get for him?" Lou asked.

"Beef prices are high. I guess about two hundred and fifty."

"Do you have a profit?"

"I don't want to sell him, Lou."

"But do you have a profit?" he persisted.

"I guess so, if you don't count taxes and hay and water."

Lou patted him again, but Corporal was busy now and paid no attention. We walked back to the house, while Jeremy went to find Dee and Prince.

I decided to plunge right into my new strategy. "I've been thinking," I began, watching Lou open his briefcase and take out a legal-sized yellow pad. "What if I wrote a book about steers instead of selling them?"

"If it sold we could decuct a few expenses," Lou conceded.

"Then that's the answer," I said. "Books on ranching are always in demand, but I have to keep the steers here. They're my subjects." I was warming up now. Lou was cooling off. "And it might make a great television series. Jeremy thinks Corporal has acting ability. We could rent him out like Lassie."

"So try it," he shrugged, writing down "250" and multiplying it by three. "How about the three new cows? Can we sell them?"

"I just bought them, Lou. Maybe next year."

"By then they'll be good actors too." He shook his head and stood up to walk in circles around me. "Well, we'll try the book and wait for peaches."

That's what I like about my accountant. He accepts defeat. The conference was ended and I was relieved. "Come on, let's go up to town for lunch. I want to tell you about the book."

"Do I need a tie?" he asked.

We drove to Solvang in the truck. It was a nice, sociable kind of day, and the tourists were out in force. Bustling from bakery to bakery, Lou enjoyed himself. The steers were not mentioned again that weekend, and I found Lou on Sunday morning out scratching Corporal's ears when I carried breakfast to the herd.

"I think I'll name one of the new calves after you," I told him.

"A cow named Lou?"

"Why not?" With Lou as his godfather he'd be safe for a couple of years. Lou leaned across the fence holding a fistfull of hay toward one of the calves. "Here Lou," he called. "Here Lou."

12

"So one morning before day, in the greatest heat of July, without acquainting anyone with his design, with all the secrecy imaginable, he...mounted his Rozinante, and at the private door of his back yard sallied out into the fields, wonderfully pleased to note with how much ease he had succeeded at the very beginning of his enterprise."
- MIGUEL DE CERVANTES

In common with the rest of my family and most of the country, the first days of summer stirred in me the annual urge to travel. My itch to be on the move, however, took a different form in my third summer of ranching and was not likely to arouse much enthusiasm in anyone else. The trip I planned would be arduous, God knows, and fraught with risk, but my destination was only five miles from the ranch. In short, I made up my mind that if I was ever to rise to the Western challenge, if I hoped to take my place as an equal in my adopted land, it was high time I climbed on a horse. At last I owned a mount emotionally and physically suited to my abilities, a horse I could trust. With Prince I felt secure, for only in dire emergency had he ever trotted, yet from a distance he looked like a real horse.

And where but to the Pancake House would I ride? Where else would my triumph be appreciated? Where else could I depend on my friends to help me to the counter after a long and dangerous journey? My mind was made up, and I announced my travel plans to Jeremy.

"But you've never been on a horse," she said, giggling her silly girlish giggle.

"I certainly have. You weren't old enough to remember Chestnut. There was a horse!"

"I better ride along on Dee."

"You're welcome if you can get up early enough, but it won't be necessary."

"You ought to get new shoes for Prince before you go."

"I intend to buy new shoes for both of us," I told her. "I've got it all worked out."

"And send us all postcards from Solvang," my daughter added.

A few riding lessons can give some people quite a sense of superiority. I sat down to make out a list of things I would need on the trip.

How fortunate animals are to have been spared man's knowledge of his own finite future and theirs! If we were not certain that we will die, would advancing age be of such concern? Would our stiffening joints feel quite as stiff? My dog is old, in the final two or three years of his life as a collie's life is usually measured, and his muzzle is grey. He rises more slowly in the morning or when there is something he must chase, and a few small front teeth are missing. When he meets a puppy that wants to play, Fernando becomes a puppy for a while, and only when the younger dog loses interest and moves on does my dog sink down to catch his breath. A little ignorance of our unimportance is not so dangerous. It allows a lovely day to end without sadness and a new one to begin with joy.

A new horse has joined our community, and the word is out that he cost his owner forty thousand dollars. The owner, whom I have not yet met, bought the Pomfit house for, I believe, less than

143

forty thousand, and out in front, in the dusty paddock surrounded by an electric fence, is the forty-thousand-dollar horse. We are all impressed, for no one else worth that much lives anywhere near us. Animals are not aware, either, of the price tag man puts on each of them. Imagine how complicated human society would become, if like animals, each of us bore a tag, not for what we own but for who we are, subject to change, of course, depending upon age and condition and clearance sales. I have never met a man I could have called a forty-thousand-dollar man, but I have just met such a horse. He was badly in need of grooming, and he was drinking hard water out of a two-dollar trough.

My one-hundred-dollar horse, Prince, met the forty-thousand-dollar horse when, one July morning, they rubbed noses above the electric fence, and neither showed any awareness of class distinction. I know because it was my first morning of our fitness program to prepare us for the long journey to the Pancake House. It was perfectly obvious to both me and Prince that we were in no condition for a five-mile ride and that a little conditioning was in order. My first move was to put our heavy Western saddle on the old horse, who so far had worn nothing heavier than a bareback pad and a twelve-year-old girl. Tossing the ponderous saddle on Prince was like tossing it over a loose clothesline. As it came down on his back, he sagged in the middle so badly that the saddle lay in a deep valley between his long, humped middle and his bony, orange hindquarters. He pulled himself together, however, and stood patiently while I followed the saddle. Then we rested.

I had timed my tryout to coincide with Jeremy's riding lesson, so there was only Fernando to watch as I kicked Prince gently into action. He took a step, then waited for me to get off. I nudged another step out of him and we were in the driveway when he stopped again. All I hoped for that first day was to get to the end of the dirt road, so I flapped my heels against Prince's flanks and off we went up the road, Prince reproachful at discovering that a man my age knew no better than to climb on his back, I somewhat dizzy whenever I looked down at the road beneath. We made it to the forty-thousand-dollar horse, however, and turned back to the stable. That was enough for one day. The next Saturday we would push on to the white bull at the corner.

My costume for the big ride was simple, colorful, unassuming. My hat, of course, came first, for there would be many horizons to squint at. Then a bright yellow Western shirt so that I was plainly visible to passing cars, Western dungarees with my freshly polished silver-dollar belt buckle and a pair of Indian boots, easy to remove, which I thought gave me the carefree yet determined look of an Apache warrior. For Prince I chose an Indian saddle blanket which covered his lump nicely and a rope to hang on the saddle. (You never know when a rope will come in handy when you are far from home.) I also bought him new shoes, and he slept while they were being nailed on. It takes more than a few nails in the foot to disturb my horse. I considered carrying a canteen and other supplies, but because our route took us past two supermarkets and several bakeries I decided against the extra weight. I wanted to travel fast and light.

The Saturday I chose was the last one in July. The time of departure - six thirty, when the sun was just up. I figured that a man can walk four miles an hour, Prince, allowing for breakdowns and rests, could walk two, which would allow two and one half hours to reach the Pancake House, getting us there at nine. I awoke at six, dressed from hat down, and moved silently in my Indian boots to the corral, where thanks to my silence and the early hour, I surprised the steers for the first time. There they were, groggy with sleep, unable to believe that I was up before they were. I led Dee and Prince into the corral for a quick snack, then returned for my own breakfast, Jeremy and a girl friend were fast asleep, so I left a note:

> **Have gone to Pancake House.**
> **Riding old Prince. Steers fed.**
> **Yours, Paul Revere**

Leaving Fernando shut in, I returned and saddled Prince, who that sunny morning looked like a great dandelion, the rising sun through his coat like a horse halo. He followed me out of the stable without a whimper and stood while I climbed on and settled myself. Then off we walked up the dirt road, moving loosely along toward the forty-thousand-dollar horse. It was a beautiful morning, the temperature, as some ancient chronicler of Valley weather once wrote, "imperceptible," the grass sparkling. A circling hawk, or perhaps it was my owl, looked down on us and went his way, and in the noiseless morning the squeak of saddle leather was the only sound. At the electric fence we stopped briefly to rest and pass a silent time of day with our expensive friend. Then on to the highway and the great world.

Almost immediately we encountered our first hazard. Just beyond the point where our dirt road meets the paved road going north, a field of alfalfa was being irrigated, and as so often happens, one of the rainbirds had been knocked out of alignment so that a stream of water sprayed across the road. I decided to stay far to the right, along Mr. Abott's walnut grove, to avoid the shower, but as we were passing under the walnut trees a light plane zoomed in to spray them. Suddenly we were buried in a cloud of strong-smelling mist as it spread above the trees, then settled to the ground. I had never heard Prince cough before. I had never, as a matter of fact, seen his right eye water, only his left. We emerged from the cloud into the sunlight again, damp, disinfected, but determined.

Our progress along the road was steady. We passed three sheep without incident, and an old man traveling to work on his tractor waved at us and cut his motor in deference to my high-spirited steed, who plodded on without turning an orange hair. We paused to rest again beside a tomato field where I lit my pipe and slumped in the saddle while Prince closed his eyes and breathed evenly. Just then two boys in a dune buggy appeared, going our way, and passed us. Their racuous shout, "Get a horse!" seemed hilarious to them, but I saw nothing particularly humorous about it. I gave them a steely stare as they disappeared down the road, then patted Prince awake. Farther along we met the first real test of my horsemanship. On the dirt path beside the road, coming toward us at high speed, was a small girl on a pony. Young and reckless, with no regard for the rules of the road, she headed straight for

Prince, who by this time had stopped, braced for the collision. At the last moment the pony veered off into high grass where the girl fell off. Now she was crying and her pony was trotting off to graze.

"You pushed me off the path," she said, sobbing and brushing at her clothes.

"You shouldn't try to play chicken with that fugitive from a merry-go-round," I told her.

"You can just catch him for me," she ordered, sniffling.

I dismounted and untied my rope from its leather thong on the saddle. While the girl watched I approached her pony from the rear, holding my rope at the ready. When I was a couple of feet from his tail I threw a might loop of rope over the whole pony and pulled. The pony, wrapped in rope, just stood there grazing. I walked over to the little girl, handed her my end of the rope, and calmly lit my pipe. The girl hauled in the pony.

When the girl was up on the pony's back again, still sniffling a little but none the worse for her fall, she turned to me, "You sure can rope horses," she said.

"Always glad to 'blige," I said, looping my rope in place again.

I rewarded Prince with a sugar lump and headed for the high school at the corner. We were behind schedule, having taken an hour and a half for the first two miles, but by pushing we might make up the time. Just before we came to the high school we passed the tennis courts where two girls were batting a ball back and forth. A wild swipe by one of the girls sent the ball over the high fence to bounce along in front of Prince, unnerving him so that he reared back. As he did so the saddle slipped to the right, and I suddenly found myself riding his rib cage, clinging to a lump on his neck and slipping fast. There was nothing to do but fall off.

The girls ran off the court to the road. While one retrieved the ball, the other held Prince's reins.

"Your horse doesn't like tennis, I guess," the girl holding Prince laughed.

"He's never played," I told her.

"Better keep your cinch tight," she advised.

While I slowly straightened up, she pulled the saddle back into position and tightened the strap under Prince's belly. "Shall I help you on again?"

"If you wouldn't mind cupping your hands," I snapped, climbing on myself from the wrong side and settling into the saddle. The girls returned to the court, and Prince and I took a short-cut across the high school lawn, leaving large, deep hoof prints in the turf. I flapped my heels as we hit the main road to Solvang.

A couple of hundred yards beyond the high school is a market where I planned to stop. The checkers there know me, and I thought it would be fun to stop for a paper, Prince waiting outside the door while I moseyed inside. But we were behind schedule so I simply rode up to the glass doors, waved, and moved on. I hoped they recognized me. On we went, along the edge of the highway now, while the early morning traffic narrowly missed us. Prince seemed to be slowing down. The next stretch was downhill, curving to the edge of the town, and we made it simply because old Prince had to move his feet to keep from falling on his nose. At the foot of the hill where traffic is warned to slow down to thirty-five miles an hour we stopped.

The town of Solvang sits on a natural stage, a platform raised above the floor of the Valley where the Danish folk opera which has been running since 1911 is performed daily for an audience of tourists. Prince and I, therefore, had to climb the eastern banks of Solvang and enter the main street of the town by passing the mission and the police station. We made our way along the mission fence to the town's only traffic light, which was red, so I pulled Prince to a stop. Of course, when the light turned green Prince remained stopped, his eyes closed, and no amount of heel gouging could start him again. While the gas-station attendants on the corner watched, I dismounted and pulled Prince through the intersection, fortunately empty at that early hour, and because we seemed to be doing so well I continued to lead him into town. We walked past the hardware store and the feed store to the small public park, where I climbed aboard again. It wouldn't do to arrive at the Pancake House dragging my horse behind me like a recalcitrant puppy.

I rode the last block, tipping my hat courteously to the girls dressed in Danish costumes on their way back to work. As we arrived at our destination, I noticed a small knot of early-rising tourists standing opposite the Pancake House, cameras at the ready.

"Hey, Mom," a small boy shouted. "A cowboy! Look, a cowboy!"

Obligingly, Prince and I paused while they took our picture. I dismounted and pulled Prince to a post outside the Pancake House where I tied the reins securely, not that he was likely to go anywhere. He looked exhausted.

My moment had arrived. I entered the Pancake House, tossed my hat to a hook on the wall and swaggered to a stool. A couple of the boys were there, reading the financial pages of the morning paper, their coffee cooling in front of them. Mrs. Santangelo saved the day.

"Just ride in from the ranch?" she asked, for Prince was clearly visible outside the windows, head down, eyes closed.

"Sure did," I said loudly. "I'd like to water my horse if you don't mind."

The cowboys looked up from their papers, nodded to me and stared out at Prince as if they had never seen a horse before. "How far d'ya come?" a man I didn't recognize asked.

Mrs. Santangelo returned with coffee for me and water for Prince in one of those cardboard cookie buckets.

"Out Refugio a ways," I allowed. (In this situation I thought it best to "allow.") I turned then and carried the water to Prince. More tourists were there admiring him, and as he sunk his nose into the cookie bucket a small boy asked me how old he was.

"He's seen a few cattle drives, sonny," I told him.

What a day!

As I turned back to have my coffee, Jim Farmer came along from his office with what appeared to be a customer. We went in together and took stools on each side of the man, who was wearing an Aloha shirt and carrying a camera.

"Say, I'd like you to meet Mr. Jenkins." We shook hands and Farmer turned to Jenkins. "Mr. Townsend owns a little ranch like you just bought."

Jenkins looked at me, impressed. "Welcome to the Valley," I told him, blinking at his shirt. "Going to put in some stock?"

Jenkins grinned uncertainly, "I guess I should," he said. "I never owned a ranch before, though."

I sipped my coffee. "Better start with permanent pasture," I suggested. "I'll be glad to come out and look the place over if you like. Or drop by my place."

"I'd sure appreciate it," Jenkins said.

"Call me any time," I told him. "My name's in the phone book."

"How's the mare," Farmer asked helpfully.

"Fine, Jim. Got her on mare and foal feed now. Thrifty little mare, all right."

Jenkins was looking at my boots appreciatively.

"Steers must be getting pretty big," Farmer observed.

"Sure are," I agreed. "About eight hundred, I'd say. Glad beef prices are up," I added, filling my pipe again.

"Is that your horse outside?" Jenkins asked.

"That's old Prince," I told him. "Rode him here for coffee."

"He's some horse."

The phone rang, and Mrs. Santangelo motioned that it was for me. It was Jeremy calling from the ranch.

"Daddy, Mrs. Schley wants to know if she should pick you up in the trailer. She's coming right by there on her way to get me and Dee."

I looked out at Prince, who seemed to be slumping. "Maybe it would be a good idea," I told her. "Call her back. I'll be out front."

I returned to finish my coffee. Farmer and Jenkins were discussing escrow and taxes, the other customers were folding their papers, preparing, I suppose, to return to their ranches. I picked up the coffee checks for the three of us and gathered my hat from the wall.

"Headin' out?" Jim asked as I walked to the cashier.

Before I could answer a small boy, the one who had insisted on getting my picture as I rode in, burst through the door.

"Mister, your horse is asleep," he shouted breathlessly, "and I think he's crying."

"Don't worry about it," I snapped. "He's not crying. His left eye runs a little."

I went out to Prince, who was asleep, and shoved a sugar lump into his jaws. He absorbed it without opening his eyes, but he did shift his weight to another leg, proving to the small crowd around him that he was alive. Nancy Schley arrived at that moment with the trailer, and I gratefully pulled Prince to the ramp, hoping to hide him before the Pancake House emptied. Up he went into the stall, but Farmer and Jenkins were watching.

"Where're you taking him, mister?" that miserable kid asked as I folded the ramp back against Prince's bottom.

"To a roundup," I called over my shoulder and ducked into the pickup.

13

"Are we tickled trout, and fools of nature?"
- EMERSON

Sometimes I wonder about nature. We are accustomed to thinking of her as a wise old female and to chastising ourselves for tampering with her plans, yet it would seem during four months of the year, here in the Valley, that nature has really fouled things up. September and October are the two hottest months, and they come, like the final supreme explosion of a skyrocket, after four hot, dry months. September and October bring searing heat to plants already tired of sun, plants fully grown and with nothing left to give, crying out now for rest. And water, the unfailing stimulant in earlier months, no longer works its magic. While the grass in the pasture seems to cry, "Leave me alone," the sun shines more feverishly than ever and I pour more gallons of water over the land at night. The earth's chemicals, which must pass through the vegetable to reach the animal, find their way suddenly blocked at their end of the chain, while at the other end voracious appetites of grazing animals continue unabated. Between the searching jaws of the herbivores and the earth's supply of nutrients, nature's converter, the plant, just quits. The result in my pasture by the end of

October is frustration.

Then, to compound this lapse in the production line, dear old nature presents us with the two coldest months of the year, capping the bones of weary plants with ice. November and December bring nightly frosts, seldom relieved by rain. Deer descend from the mountains, hoping that things are arranged more sensibly in the valleys. Cattle wait at feed bins, let down by nature, their last hope in man.

These four mixed-up months in our calendar brought about the first real crisis on the Townsend ranch. We were beginning our fourth year as the sun baked the pasture to a crisp and the frost quick-froze the remnants. Eight animals stood in the barn, mouths watering, like cats waiting at abandoned mouseholes. And not a drop of rain fell. There was nothing for the rancher to do but forage for hay, a commodity, I discovered, which is in plentiful supply when the grass is high and almost nonexistent when it is needed. As if they sensed a dry winter, the ranchers in the Valley who had hay decided to keep it for themselves, while those who wanted to buy were forced to decide whether it was wiser to pay for expensive hay or sell cattle cheap.

I was, of course, spared this decision, for I had a family to feed, not a bunch of black, furry commodities, to say nothing of a mare eating for two and an old horse who might chew slowly but who nevertheless chews steadily. As has so often been the case in my days as a rancher, economics could not be the deciding factor. At any price, hay must be found.

In the early weeks of the four-month panic Jeremy and I did quite well. We gathered two-dollar bales on Saturday morning from Ed McCarty's barn, we discovered a few bales behind Mattei's Tavern and carried them home, we scrounged a ton of old alfalfa from a nearby ranch because it was too old to feed high-priced horses. We returned each Saturday to the ranch with whatever we could buy to be greeted by bellows from the waiting herd. I began to feel like a harassed robin in a wormless world, staring into eight gaping mouths. Still the drought continued.

We spent Thanksgiving, then Christmas in a world without grass. No longer did the steers come to the corral fence at sunrise and sunset for food, devoting the rest of the day to roaming the pasture and resting along the fence line. Now, deprived of what must have seemed to them a basic bovine right to graze, they stood around all day, waiting for hay, as the hollows deepened around their bony haunches. Even the horses were waiting at the gate in the morning. Dee rounded with foal, Prince rounded only with fluff.

It was confidently forecasted that January would bring rain. "Watch for the wind to shift into the east," I was advised, but my immovable weather vane still pointed stubbornly west. Magnus Jepson's stump always pained him before a rain, but there was no discomfort and no rain. My pregnant horse, I was told, must have green grass, but even in the garden, where grass appears first, there was none, so I made arrangements with Jim Farmer to move Dee to a pasture at his ranch watered by a brook and still green. There she would stay until her foal arrived in February, while Prince and I and Jeremy got along on our wasted acres. Our supply of hay sources was dwindling.

Shortly after Dee left for her final weeks we had a night of rain. I awoke to hear the trickling sound from the eaves, and in the morning the surface of our world was damp and alive again. But it was a light rain, a deceiving spring to awaken roots and create a mossy surface on the hills. A week of sunshine left the Valley parched again, the false start baked out of the ground almost before we could see its effect.

Meanwhile, a foal was coming. Every Saturday afternoon Jeremy went to visit Dee, walking her around the pasture, brushing her and watching the great swelling in her stomach drop lower. And while Jeremy soothed the mare, I prepared for her family. The corral must be fenced with close-meshed wire, so my one-handed fence builder and I spent a Saturday pulling and stretching the wire from post to post. Prince followed us around, interested. The paper bag filled with staples was, to Corporal, the closest thing to lunch he had seen in several weeks, so he reached under the rails and made off with it. Chasing a steer that's holding a bag of staples in his mouth is a foolish thing for a grown man to be doing on a Saturday afternoon. My inclination to explain to him that staples aren't good for big strong steers was, of course, wasted, so we romped across the pasture, Corporal like a puppy with a sock, I brandishing my hammer at him. Magnus just laughed.

Next we built a manger in one of the stalls, so that Dee and her son (we were certain it would be a colt) could eat something during the week. I watered the corral at night, hoping to grow a stand of grass there at least. A vision of the Curragh Stock Farm remained in my mind, where a mare with a spindly foal lived in deep grass, her milk rich, her offspring glossy. Now a year later there was no grass, and a new horse was about to step into a world no longer inclined to support him.

I calculated that by the time Dee's foal arrived, the cost for my "free foal" would run about as follows:

Boarding fees at stock farm	$125.00
Vet bills	$ 35.00
Mare & foal feed (8 months)	$ 50.00
Fence & manger materials	$120.00
Extra salt lick	$ 1.50
Total	$331.50

This amount, exclusive of my labor, Magnus's and Dee's is more than eleven times what it cost Thoreau to build his house in 1845, and he splurged on such things as "hair" and "chalk." But then I have excluded carrots and shampoo, which I suppose were not really necessary.

The weeks between mid-January and Valentine's Day, which was my choice for foaling day, were spent in anticipation, indecision, and inaction. In short, I stood around a lot. For the first time in more than three years I noticed fountains of water starting up in dry fields around me as other ranchers gave up their wait for rain. I looked at my pipes and wondered. I rationed hay, not knowing where to find more, and I substituted lots of nose scratching and commiseration with my hungry herd, looking out at the miserable contours of what should have been permanent pasture, now a brown, bumpy terrain forsaken even by gophers. To begin irrigation in January would add two hundred dollars to my water bill for the year, in addition to my hay bill, which was already approaching catastrophe. To hold off the water might mean a summer of starvation. Was this really Marlboro country? Did Cole Porter really say, "Let me ride to the ridge where the West commences/Gaze at the moon till I lose my senses?" What would he do now when his old "cayuse" was so hungry he was trying to unzip his tobacco pouch?

As foaling time approached, I knew the tension in Jeremy was mounting. She is a quiet girl, and she limited her own signs of anxiety over Dee to scrubbing her coat for hours, walking with her in the green grass of the Farmer pasture, her head bent like Dee's, wishing for the arrival. No new animal had ever been born in Jeremy's short life, and, I am certain, the mystery of births occupied her thoughts. "Does she lie down?" Jeremy asks. "Do you think it will happen at night?" Dee's straining flanks, the gradual waxing over of her milk bag were signs Jeremy had been told about, and she had been worried too by masses of information freely offered by all our friends. "You better hope it's not twins," she was told. "One is never any good." Jeremy tried to smile. "Just so long as it comes out head first," somebody said, leaving the alternative for my daughter to worry about. "I just hope I'm here when she has it," Jeremy told me. Then she announced her foal shower.

On a Saturday afternoon in Los Angeles a group of Jeremy's classmates arrived for the shower, each bringing a gift. Their shower was spent listening to records and talking softly in another room of the house, but when it was over and mothers were picking up daughters, I came out to find a table filled with bunches of carrots, piles of sugar cubes, and a box of oatmeal. The new arrival was due in a week.

February 12 was the first day, by my calculations, that the foal could arrive. A nice Lincoln's Birthday sort of foal. But there was no call from Farmer, so nothing happened.

Jeremy and I were at the ranch on Valentine's Day, a perfect day for a foal to arrive. Dee stood in the far corner of the Farmer pasture, head down, bulging, occasionally nipping her flank as, I suppose, her heir gave her a swift kick from inside. But nothing happened.

Certain a foal would arrive the following week, Jeremy and I made elaborate arrangements, beginning with a promised phone call from Farmer. Then I would call Jeremy's school, proclaim an emergency, take her out of class, and run for the ranch. Each day passed with no phone call.

We arrived back in Santa Ynez for the Washington's Birthday weekend, a perfect time for the foal to arrive because we had Monday off. Freddie, Susie, and Nicole drove up on Saturday to visit the new arrival, so we all stood with Dee while she nibbled hay, the foal still uncomfortably tucked inside her. Jeremy and I waited most of Sunday. No foal.

The phone rang. It was Lou, in San Francisco, asking whether I had sold anything. We arranged to spend the holiday in Los Angeles working on my taxes. I told him I might have to leave if the foal arrived. It didn't.

I bought a few carrots to pass out to my friends. They wilted on my desk, turning rubbery the way carrots do. Jeremy went back to school complaining of a stomach ache.

On the twenty-fifth of February at nine thirty in the morning Jim Farmer called. "Well, you had a foal this morning," he said. "Born at six fifteen."

"How is it, what is it?"

"You got a little colt. He's find. Up having his breakfast now. He's a cream-colored Palomino with a white blaze like his mother."

"How's Dee?"

"She's fine. No problem. Didn't even have to call the vet."

"Thanks, Jim," I said. "Thanks for the good news."

I sat back in my office chair. Eleven months and ten days after Joe the Teaser found Dee the Ready Mare a horse had been born on the Townsend ranch. Up there where I loved so much to be, a small colt the color of a coffee milkshake was trying out his new legs, alive and alert to a world of soft, sweet air. His father, probably off on his rounds of teasing, would never know he existed, but I would. I did. His life would probably stretch far beyond my own, but Jeremy would somehow find a way to keep him in the family.

I called the school. "I'd like to leave a message for my daughter, Jeremy Townsend."

"What's the message," a businesslike female voice asked.

"Tell her that a Palomino colt was born this morning, mother and son are doing well."

"Is this an emergency?" the woman asked.

"No," I said, "but she'll want to know."

"We'll tell her," the voice said, softer now.

14

"We behold the face of nature bright with gladness..."
- CHARLES DARWIN

To leave home at the start of a vacation trip must be for all of us a moment in life which, like Christmas morning, never loses its special flavor. With house locked, luggage packed away beside us, the ride down our familiar street, then the sudden turn away from town and school and office, outwardbound, confirms that this day is like no other and that everything so worth waiting for is suddenly about to happen. How fortunate Jeremy and I have been now for more than three years, for this looking forward to, this final departure toward, fulfillment is our weekly experience. Our leaving for the ranch seems always to hold new promises. I cannot remember a week when we sighed with the effort it would take.

Few Fridays were quite like this one, however. There was the weekend when we saw the steers grazing in our pasture for the first time and the Friday when Dee was waiting for us. There was the first trip in the new truck, its bed filled with Fernando. But this was out trip to the new foal, and we began it like two people who know what is inside the Christmas package, yet who expect to be delightfully surprised.

Our path to the ranch follows the coast road along the Pacific, then inland to the town of Oxnard where, for a moment, we join homeward-bound traffic. Then to the freeway past Ventura and another tangle of traffic in Santa Barbara, a city which has planted four traffic signals on the freeway, hoping, I suppose, to hold a few nomads in its clutches before we all slip through and northward. A hundred Santa Barbaras could have not detained us, for just beyond the last traffic light and over the coastal mountains was our Valley.

As we crawled through Santa Barbara the skies became suddenly dark with rain clouds, and the first sprinkles splashed the windshield. At another time, in another place, I suppose these slate clouds would be described as "threatening," but to us ranchers in the final weeks of disastrous drought they were at least promising, if not downright inspiring. As we climbed the seaward slope of the mountains rain began to fall harder, and Fernando looked in at us from the truck bed, his coat beaded with bright drops.

When we reached the summit, the rain was established, polishing smooth boulders, darkening red banks of clay on either side of us, rippling the road ahead with new water. I had lived long enough under Western skies to rejoice with all living things at the start of the first soaking rain. No system of irrigation invented by man to catch and carry water from one place to another can accomplish the miracle of fresh rain falling on the land. No tantalizing mist of morning can so arouse our Valley. The long wait was over, the false starts behind us. Now the rain fell at last in tall gray curtains.

The ride down into the Valley from the cloud-capped peak where once the Concord stages paused to rest weary horses before rolling on to Los Olivos and Mattei's Tavern was made in ever-increasing rain. Waving to Fernando to be patient I drove faster. Now we could see the Valley floor. Soon we would be turning into the ranch. Then a pause to unload, pitch a hay stack to the steers, and head for the Farmer ranch. Rain and a new foal, all in one day.

Jim Farmer's ranch is appropriate to a man who has spent a

lifetime in the West, half a lifetime in the Valley. Flanked by pastured hills spotted with cattle and horses, the heart of the Farmer ranch lies in a triangular ravine, at the apex of which is his modern ranch house. Immediately below the house is the small Farmer lake, and just beyond the lake is the pasture, white-fenced and green, where a spring of brook divides and waters it. From a hundred yards down the road in the driving rain Jeremy and I could see Dee, standing beneath a leafless tree, her dark, wet, body barely concealing a small white form beside her.

"I see him," cried Jeremy as we drove along the pasture to the tree.

Ignoring the rain, we jumped from the truck and ran to the fence to be greeted as always by Dee, as never before by her new son. The colt, a wobbly, inept replica of a horse, like a child's first attempt to draw one, with body too small, legs too long, head all wrong, advanced beside his mother, afraid of us, more afraid to be left behind. Rain had washed away whatever soft outlines he possessed, coursing down four knobby legs that must belong to an older horse, for he walked on them like a girl in her first high heels. A white brush tail was tucked between his buttocks, a white mop mane dripped more water, and the scruffy beginnings of a white goatee gave his face the appearance of an aging rocking horse. As Jeremy climbed the fence to approach him, he whinnied, the bewildered cry of the new arrival who had expected something better than a cold shower.

I shall never forget that first glimpse of our first-born horse. Darkness was approaching fast under rain-filled clouds. Dee, darker still and heavy from recent birth, stood with us, nuzzling for food, while the colt stood out beside her like an iridescent wraith, whiter because everything around him was deep brown, the way grass looks greener in the darkness of a thunder storm. Wet as he was we could distinguish the white socks on his long legs, the white blaze between his dark eyes.

"He's going to be a Palomino," I told Jeremy. "And he's beautiful."

She did not answer. With one hand on Dee's wet back she

161

reached slowly down to the trembling colt's slim neck and lightly ran her hand along his back. He stood, allowing her to touch him for a moment before shrinking against his mother. Then he put his head under her belly and sucked violently, legs splayed, small white hooves anchored in mud.

It was too dark, too wet to remain there. Jeremy and I got into the truck and drove slowly back down the road, she looking back at mother and son.

"He looks so cold," Jeremy said.

"We'll bring him home tomorrow," I promised.

The trickle of water from the eaves continued through the night, so strange a sound that it wakened me several times, so comforting that I went back to sleep again. With morning the rain continued in sporadic showers, sinking into the lawn and pasture as no man-made rain could ever do, forming small puddles on pads of earth packed by the hooves of cattle. Between showers the sudden croak of a frog that had found its voice in this newly lubricated world was answered on the far side of the lawn by another scraping croak, then another as the stereophonic chorus continued in joyous agreement. Steers fed, breakfast finished, Jeremy and I called Nancy Schley for help with the great crosstown adventure. She would meet us at the Farmer ranch at eleven. We set out, stopping only long enough to buy a small halter and lead rope for the colt, knowing it would be weeks before he would consent to wear them.

We arrived to find the Schleys already waiting, so Jeremy slipped a halter on Dee and led her slowly down the path to the trailer, her son moving behind her, a thin, white shadow in the pouring rain. With one worried glance behind to make sure the colt was with her, Dee moved into the trailer and was boarded up for the trip home. Slowly we moved through the town so our family would not slip as corners were turned. Slowly we drove into the ranch and parked near the corral. Then Dee and her foal moved out of the trailer and into the stable where I had prepared her manger, filled now with warm, dry hay. In fits and starts, like a nervous fawn, the colt adjusted to his new home, standing when Dee stood, leaping to catch up when Dee moved. The rain continued.

My mission accomplished, my clothes soaked, I retired to the house for the rest of the day to listen to the welcome water. Jeremy remained in the stable where she sat on a bale of hay next to Dee and the colt, toweling Dee now and then, wiping away the rain from her own hair with the same towel. Not until late that afternoon when I again went to the stable for more hay for the steers would Jeremy agree to come in and dry off. Prince, blissfully drenched at the far end of the pasture, never knew of our arrival and never came down to visit.

At Mattei's Jeremy and I were greeted with congratulations. "What are you going to call him?" Betty McClelland asked.

"I guess I'll call him Mattei," Jeremy said, whereupon whoops of pleasure came from all who knew us there. Old Felix Mattei looked down from the wall, stern-faced and dignified, as he was being immortalized, and we drank a toast to the new Mattei. We drove home in heavy rain and after checking the stables where Dee and Mattei stood on the only dry land for miles around, we went to bed, the streams of water still splashing the cement walk outside my window, making crackling sounds like dry wood burning.

Why does the West, and its personification, the cowboy, nourish dreams, excite imaginations, even arouse fond envy in men like me? What is there about a painting by Charles Russell, the history of an early Western settlement, even the trite plot of a television Western that puts a faraway look in our eyes? For one thing, I believe the charisma of the cowboy is explained by his relationship to the rest of life around him. He was closer to and more affected by natural forces than most men, and he developed a respect for nature's laws at a time when there was little need and less respect for those of men. His most valuable possession was an animal, a horse on which he spent most of his life, his dependence upon, and therefore his appreciation for a cow pony make him appealing. And he was not a sure winner in the struggle for survival

163

in nature. His enemies, thirst, heat and cold, other animals are the enemies of other living things.

Most of all, I think, the cowboy lived in an environment many of us long to share with him. There was little between him and the horizon and, increasingly, this spacious setting for his life seems desirable. The West still offers, here and there, vistas empty of humanity and its traces of occupancy, and it is still possible to ride a horse in a straight line as far as he will go. In our Valley there are still more animals than people, more trees than houses, more fields than lawns. It is possible today for a man to get lost in our mountains, and, when I think of it, that is a fine thing.

What happens when any living thing in the chain of life loses its last enemy and is no longer threatened? As Charles Darwin wrote over a century ago, by overpopulation of its environment a living organism becomes its own enemy and destroys itself. Is man, thinking man, immune from this law of nature? I do not believe so, yet today architects, learning from the ant and the bee, those ultimate socialists, confidently plan the structures in which we will be able to live in smaller, more efficient spaces; chemists work to feed the world, anticipating the approaching time when all natural food is gone.

Here in the Valley we live on the shores of a spreading human sea, stretching from San Diego to Santa Barbara. To the east the plans are already complete to bring water to the desert so that mass-man can live where no man has lived. Like the grizzly fleeing ever northward we keep moving out of the way of ourselves, even taking the leap into outer space, only to discover the terrifying fact that, as ancient men believed, we are the center of our universe, that at the edge of earth life stops. As we all now stare with new knowledge at the moon, we must turn with new concern to the earth.

Men who feel as I do, who like to join the cowboy in spirit as he rides alone, will continue to come West in search of the remnants of its once-challenging canvas of wilderness. How much longer they will find an untouched corner none of us knows, but concievably within the life of Jeremy's new colt there will no longer be room for him in the Valley. His pasture will become a hundred "building pads" and off he will go, tail tucked between his legs, in a trailer heading north.

I believe my Sunday behavior on the ranch has corresponded with the pattern of all country dwellers during the hundred and fifty Sundays at the Townsend ranch. Like theirs, my Sunday begins like any other day, early, and continues until my steers and horses are fed. Then Sunday changes. It becomes a day for admiring what I have accomplished on Saturday, and that can as often as not be done flat on my back. While Jeremy takes her Sunday ride up the road, I take stock of the improvements I have brought about in one day's labor. Nothing new is begun on Sunday. Nothing, if it has any consideration, goes wrong. Then, by noon we close up the house, boot Fernando into the truck, and turn down the road to Los Angeles.

Today is Sunday, Mattei's first Sunday. When I awoke the rain was slanting across the lawn in long gray lines, so that I bent against it on my trip to the corral. Dee and her soaked little foal were there in the dark stable, the cattle at the trough, waiting. I carried hay in three loads to them, pitching it over my new wire fence, hoping they would dispose of it before it was too wet to eat, for my herd is fussy. They do not eat hay they have walked on, or hay that has been rained on. Dee followed me out with each forkful, stealing bites as I carried the hay, and Mattei, who like all young animals with extra energy never seems to walk in a straight line, zigzagged behind us. Then I brought a bowl of grain to Dee, while Mattei enjoyed his breakfast farther back, and Fernando, who loves mare and foal feed, waited for Dee to spill some. Then it was time to stretch out inside the house.

Jeremy appeared and fixed her breakfast. I watched her walk slowly to the stable, rain streaking her long blonde hair, her heavy jacket pulled protectively around her. The rain continued through the morning, and we were reluctant to leave our new colt to the dismal day. I went back once to the corral this morning to find Mattei curled up in the mud beside his mother, dozing at the water trough, resigned, I suppose, to the obvious fact that in this new world rain was never ending. Jeremy stood with Dee, both dripping, both looking fondly at Mattei.

"Let's stay for lunch," I suggested. "Maybe the sun will come out before we have to go."

We made soup for ourselves at noon and watched the sky. It seemed to be separating into smaller bundles, and at the rim of the Valley, spreading across the foothills, a long, golden streak of sunlight appeared. From my window I watched the streak broaden over distant fields, moving toward us in a golden tide. I saw Dee turn her head toward the light, and Mattei, standing close, followed her gaze and watched the sun move toward him. We waited.

It was after one o'clock when the sun reached Mattei, but it was a lovely moment, as if he had been finally welcomed, finally acknowledged. Suddenly he stood there, bright in the center of the stage, blinking his eyes in the light, sniffing self-consciously at all this heavenly attention. Then, twitching his toothbrush tail, he kicked up his heels and off he went without his mother, convinced now that it was good to be alive.

Of his escape from the city to the woods, Thoreau wrote, "I learned this at least, by my experiment; that if one advances confidently in the direction of his dreams, and endeavors to live the life he has imagined, he will meet with a success unexpected in common hours." Thoreau was not a weekend woodsman as I have been a weekend rancher, and he probably would have scoffed (I am not certain Thoreau ever laughed) at my experiment. But then Thoreau was young and alone. He had no need to consider anyone but himself, as I still have. Yet, I believe that today, as Jeremy and I prepare to leave the ranch for another week, I can echo his words. I believe I too have met with a "Success unexpected in the common hours," and that I am better for it.

Scientists from Darwin to Eiseley have recognized the existence of islands in nature where the unique develop and the unfittest survive, where the great changes in the chain of life evolve. But such islands are not alone for those who make a significant genetic contribution. The earthly inheritance of the meek occurs there, and none should be denied a passport to his island. For me the ranch has been such an island. It has been a place of challenge without threat, of struggle without defeat. It has been a place to think and, I think, to know. It has also been a refuge for others. It has been the final protection from neglect for an old horse and the first enveloping assurance for a new one. For Jeremy, like me, it has been a place to learn.

My island is not without conflict. The badger blasts the gopher, the hawk still circles the mouse. But then, there are many islands, and, perhaps, mine is not theirs.

THE END

EPILOGUE

The following Saturday the sun shone. Mattei, curled in the mud, felt secure in his mother's shadow, while Jeremy and I stopped watching long enough to eat lunch. The phone rang.

"It's for you," Jeremy said. "Somebody wants to know if this is the Townsend ranch."

I grabbed the phone. "Yes," I said. "Yes, it is."

"This is Mr. Jenkins. Jim Farmer introduced us."

"Oh, yes," I enthused. I had no idea who he was, but already I liked him.

"You offered to show me your ranch, give me a little advice. Is the offer still good?"

"Come right on over," I told him. "I'll be glad to show you around." Now I remembered Jenkins. At the Pancake House. A finer fellow I never met.

The Townsend ranch! It had taken almost three years and a tenderfoot in an Aloha shirt to do it, but, by God, we had done it! Now I could have one of those small, neat signs made to hang over the mailbox. Perhaps in walnut, very Spanish, with our brand burned into the wood. I shook hands with Jeremy. I shook hands with Fernando.

Jenkins showed up in the middle of my nap, dressed now in new Western clothes, and he got the grand tour. I walked him around the pasture, demonstrating my pipes, giving advice on fencing, explaining the habits of gophers and badgers. The steers followed us wherever we went, making Jenkins a little jumpy, but I reassured him by shouting "Ho" and pushing Corporal's nose out of his pocket. The ranch looked better that day than it had ever looked, as Jenkins and I stood later on my lawn looking out over the land, the herd, the horses. It seemed to me that I had always lived there and that I always would. I walked him back to his car.